RAPID
INTERPRETATION
OF
EKG's

...a programmed course

By

Dale Dubin, M. D.

*All illustrations and graphic
art were produced by the author.*

Published by:
COVER Publishing Company*
P.O. Box 1092
TAMPA, FLORIDA
*a division of C.O.V.E.R. Inc.

Exclusive Foreign Publishing/Distribution Rights
granted in accordance with
Universal Copyright Convention
for
French: Librairie Maloine, France
Italian: Diffusione Edizioni Mediche Internazionali, Italy
Spanish: Interamericana, S.A. de C.V., Mexico
Japanese: Bunkodo Co., Ltd., Japan
Serbo-croatian: Sportska Knjiga, Yugoslavia
German: Springer-Verlag, Germany
Portuguese: EPUC—Editora De Publicacoes Cientificas LTDA.
Persian: Pirated Edition by Eqbal Publishing Co., Iran

Library of Congress Catalog Card Number 74-117076.
SBN 0-912912-00-6

To Those From Whom I Have Learned:

Dr. George C. Griffith
Dr. Willard J. Zinn
Dr. Henry J. L. Marriot
Dr. Charles Fisch
Dr. William L. Martz
Dr. Nathan Marcus
Dr. Richard G. Connar
Dr. Jose Dominguez
Dr. Louis Cimino
Dr. David Baumann

ACKNOWLEDGMENTS...

It gives me great pleasure to acknowledge my indebtedness:

To all my teachers from whom I have learned principles of electrocardiology.

To the Florida Regional Medical Program and the Florida Heart Association for permitting me to arrange and teach the electrocardiographic portion of their Coronary Care Training Program.

To Drs. Nathan Marcus and Arthur Stevenson for their critique and didactic assistance in preparation.

To the electrocardiography department of Tampa General Hospital for their help in obtaining pathological electrocardiograms.

To J. Thomas Dillin, Phillip Blair, and Michael J. King for the excellent photography and technical assistance.

To Miss Susan Timmes for her help in layout and proof-reading.

To Dr. Edward Spoto, chief of the Department of Cardiology at the University of South Florida School of Medicine for editorial advice on the third edition.

To my publisher, C.O.V.E.R. Publishing Company, for their great understanding and cooperation. My association with the publisher represents the closest possible concert between author and publisher.

TABLE OF CONTENTS

"To make a great dream come true, the first requirement is a great capacity to dream; the second is persistence — a faith in the dream."

Hans Selye, M. D.

Before you begin:

This book is presented as a rapid programmed course. Programmed instruction may be new to you, but don't hesitate to give it a try because it is a little different. It works; and learning progresses quickly once you become accustomed to it. But you have to follow the rules.

Start at the beginning of the book, at Frame 1. You will only lose by jumping ahead. If you progress at a steady rate, you can finish this book at a single sitting. You will be surprised at how fast you can proceed through the book. Programmed instruction must be studied carefully for it is a series of concepts, the usual wordy superfluous language has been trimmed away.

First, look at each frame carefully and read the caption. This simple task may tempt you to scan rapidly and miss detail and subtle points. Study each frame carefully and relate the caption. Cover the right column of answers with a strip of paper. Read the first statement and determine the missing word. Check your answer against the word given in the right hand column (you need not write your answer in the blank space). Do not feel disappointed if you fail to produce the correct word — there are many synonyms. This is not an examination nor are you competing with anyone for right answers.

If your word choice is markedly different from the answer given, return to the frame and study the caption again to see where you have erred. Notes are added randomly in areas where I have found that students may falter.

After you have mastered the concept that is illustrated and have correctly supplied the blank words, proceed to the next frame. At times this sequence may seem unduly simple. This generally means that the system is working. Just take your time and "play the game" as they say. You will be pleasantly surprised at how much you have learned and how quickly you can interpret electrocardiograms.

Happy learning!
Dale Dubin, M.D.

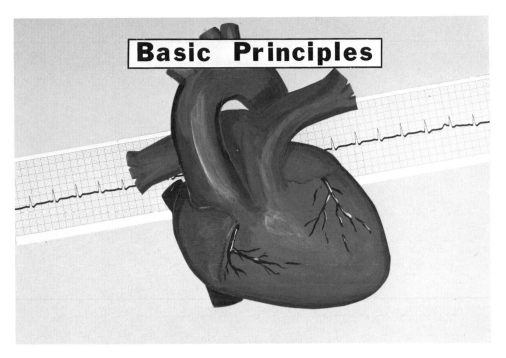

Basic Principles

The electrocardiogram (EKG) is a valuable record of the heart's function (electrical activity).

The electrocardiogram is commonly known by the three letters _____, and gives us valuable information concerning the heart's _____.

EKG

function

NOTE: For years the medical profession has used the letters EKG to represent electrocardiogram. The "K" replaces the "C" of "cardio" to avoid confusion with EEG (brain wave recording) because ECG and EEG sound alike. Some purists claim ECG is more correct, but we will continue to refer to the electrocardiogram as an EKG since this term is more common.

The electrocardiogram is inscribed on a ruled paper strip and gives us a permanent _____ of cardiac activity.

record

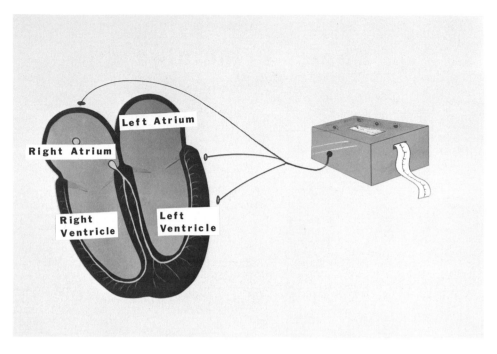

The electrocardiogram records the electrical impulses that stimulate the heart to contract.

The information recorded on the EKG represents the _____ impulses from the heart.

electrical

These electrical impulses represent various stages of cardiac _____.

stimulation

NOTE: The EKG also yields valuable information on the heart during resting and recovery phases.

When the heart muscle is electrically stimulated, it _____.

contracts

NOTE: The main purpose of this illustration is to familiarize you with the diagramatic cross section of the heart which will be used continuously throughout this book. You probably could have recognized the various chambers without the labels, but I added them anyway.

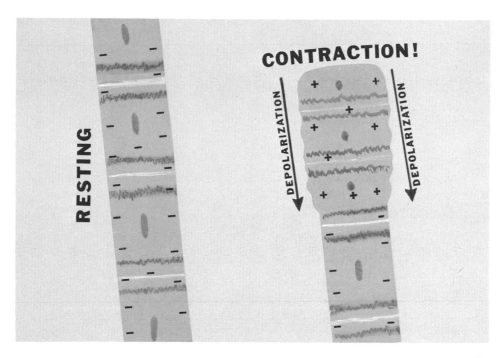

Heart cells are charged or polarized in the resting state, but when electrically stimulated, they "depolarize" and contract.

In the resting state the cells of the heart are _____;
the inside of the cells being _____ charged.

polarized
negatively

NOTE: In the strictest sense, a resting polarized cell has a
negatively charged interior and a positively charged surface.
For the sake of simplicity we will consider only the inside
of the myocardial cell.

The interiors of the myocardial cells which are usually
negatively charged become _____ly charged as the
cells are stimulated to contract.

positive

The electrical stimulation of these specialized muscle cells
is called _____ and causes them
to _____.

depolarization
contract

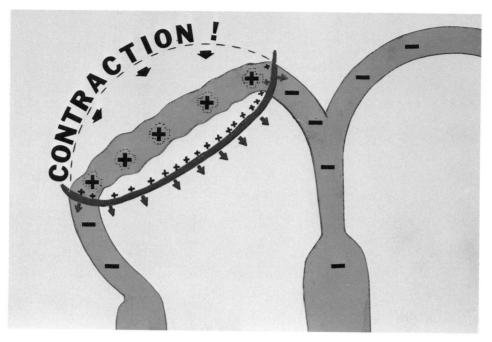

Thus a progressive wave of stimulation (depolarization) passes through the heart causing contraction of the myocardium.

This depolarization may be considered as an advancing wave of _____ charges within the cells.

positive

NOTE: Depolarization stimulates the myocardial cells to contract as the charge within each cell changes to positive.

The electrical stimulus of depolarization causes progressive contraction of the _____ cells as the wave of positive charges advances down the interior of the cells.

myocardial

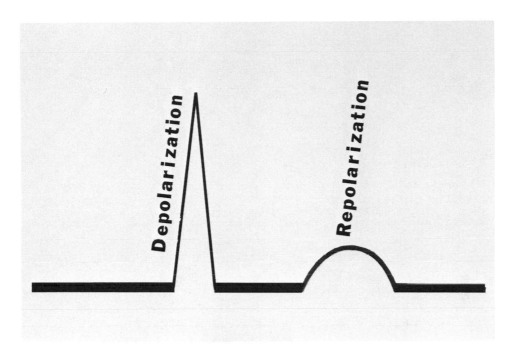

The wave of depolarization (cells become positive inside) and repolarization (cells return to negative) are recorded on the EKG as shown.

The stimulating wave of depolarization charges the interior of the myocardial cells _____.

positively

During _____ the myocardial cells regain the negative charge within each cell.

repolarization

NOTE: Repolarization is a strictly electrical phenomenon and the heart remains physically quiet during this activity.

Myocardial stimulation, or _____, and the recovery phase, or _____, are recorded on the EKG as shown.

depolarization
repolarization

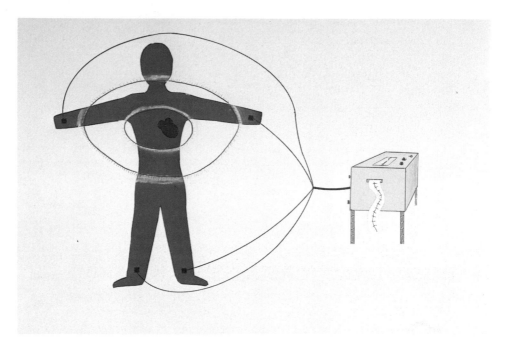

As this electrical activity passes through the heart, it may be picked up by external (skin) sensors and recorded as an EKG.

Both depolarization and repolarization are
——————— phenomena.   electrical

The electrical activity of the heart may be recorded from the ———— by sensitive monitoring equipment.   skin

The EKG records the electrical activity of the heart from electrode ———— placed on the skin.   sensors

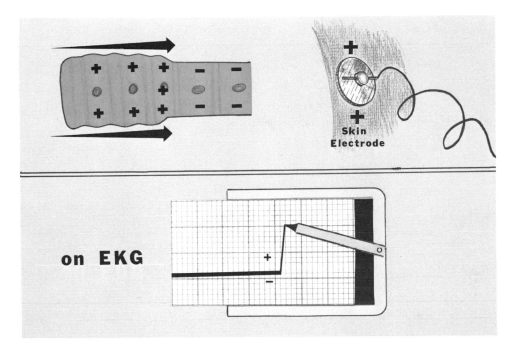

on EKG

As the positive wave of depolarization within the heart cells moves toward a positive (skin) electrode, there is a positive (upward) deflection recorded on EKG.

An advancing wave of depolarization may be considered a moving wave of _____ charges.

positive

When this wave of positive charges is moving toward a positive _____ electrode, there is a simultaneous upward deflection recorded on EKG.

skin

If you see an upward wave (of depolarization) on EKG, it means at that instant there was a depolarization stimulus moving _____ a positive skin electrode.

toward

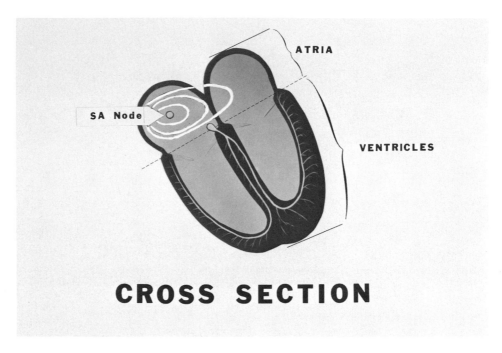

CROSS SECTION

The S A Node begins the electrical impulse which spreads in wave fashion, stimulating both atria.

The _____, located in the posterior wall of the right atrium, initiates the electrical impulse for cardiac stimulation.

S A Node

This wave of depolarization proceeds from the S A Node and stimulates both _____.

atria

As this depolarization _____ passes through the atria, it produces a concurrent wave of atrial contraction.

wave

NOTE: The electrical stimulus originating from the S A Node proceeds away from the node concentrically in all directions. If the atria were a pool of water and a pebble dropped at the S A Node, an enlarging circular wave would spread out from the S A Node. This is the manner in which atrial depolarization proceeds away from the S A Node. Remember that atrial depolarization is a spreading wave of positive charges within the myocardial cells.

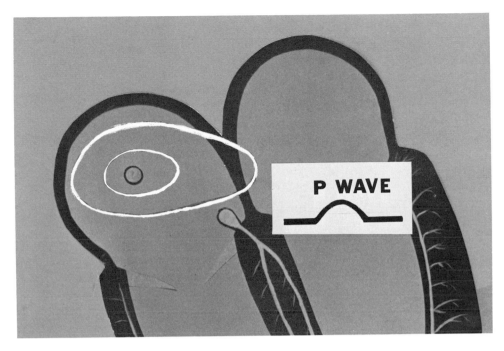

This electrical impulse spreads across the atria and yields a P wave on the EKG.

The wave of depolarization sweeping through the ＿＿＿＿＿ can be picked up by the sensitive skin sensors.   atria

This atrial stimulation is recorded as a ＿＿＿ wave.   P

The P wave represents atrial ＿＿＿＿＿＿ electrically.   depolarization
                                                                 (stimulation)

Thus the P wave represents the electrical activity of the contraction of both atria.

As the wave of depolarization passes through both atria, there is a simultaneous wave of atrial _____.

contraction

So the _____ wave represents the depolarization and contraction of both atria.

P

NOTE: In reality contraction lags slightly behind depolarization but we will consider both to be occurring simultaneously.

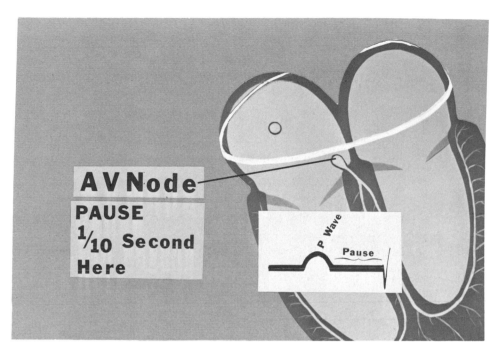

The impulse then reaches the A V Node, where there is a 1/10 second pause, allowing blood to enter the ventricles.

This stimulating wave of depolarization eventually reaches the _____.

A V Node

At the A V Node there is a 1/10 second _____ before the impulse actually stimulates the A V Node. There are many theories as to how this occurs, but we are mainly concerned with the fact that there is a pause before the A V Node is stimulated.

pause

This 1/10 second pause allows the blood to pass through the A V valves into the _____.

ventricles

NOTE: At this point we are correlating the electrical phenomena with the mechanical physiology. The atria contract forcing blood through the A V valves, but it takes a little time for the blood to travel through the valves into the ventricles (about 1/10 second).

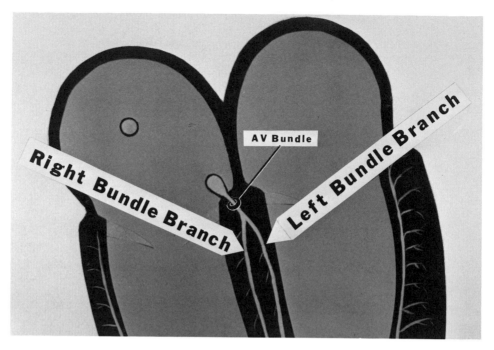

After the 1/10 second pause, the A V Node is stimulated, initiating an electrical impulse that starts down the A V Bundle into the Bundle Branches.

After this pause the _____ receives the depolarization stimulus from the atria.

A V Node

This electrical stimulus passes from the A V Node down the A V Bundle to the Left and Right _____ _____.

Bundle Branches

As the stimulus progresses away from the A V Node, this initiates ventricular _____.

depolarization

NOTE: The A V Bundle (bundle of His), which extends down from the A V Node, divides into Right and Left Bundle Branches within the interventricular septum.

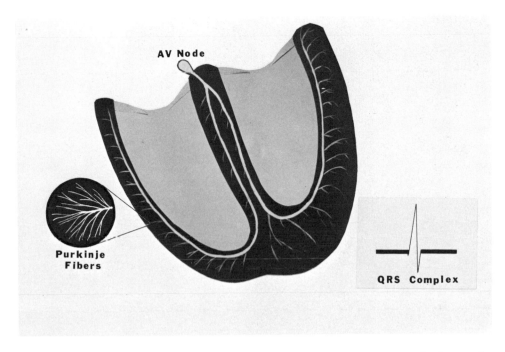

The QRS complex represents the electrical impulse as it travels from the A V Node to the Purkinje fibers and into the myocardial cells.

NOTE: The neuro-muscular conduction system of the ventricles is composed of specialized nervous material which transmits the electrical impulse from the A V Node. It is composed of the A V Node, the A V Bundle, and the Right and Left Bundle Branches which terminate in the fine Purkinje fibers. The electrical impulses travel much more rapidly through this specialized nervous tissue than is possible through the myocardial cells.

The electrical impulse travels from the _____ to the A V Bundle and then to the Right and Left Bundle Branches terminating in the Purkinje fibers.

A V Node

A _____ _____ is described on the EKG as the electrical stimulus passes from the A V Node down the ventricular conduction system terminating in the ventricular myocardial cells.

QRS complex

The QRS complex, therefore, represents the electrical activity of the stimulation of the _____.

ventricles

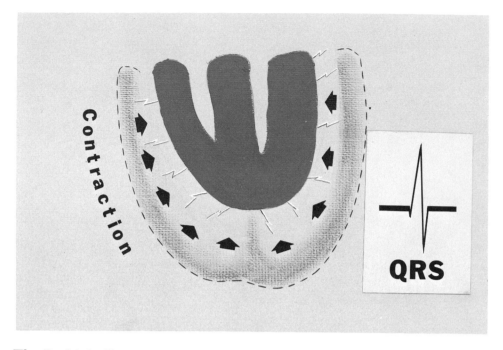

The Purkinje fibers transmit the electrical impulse to the myocardial cells causing simultaneous contraction of the ventricles.

The fine Purkinje fibers transmit the _____ stimulus directly to the myocardial cells.

electrical

When this impulse reaches the _____ cells of the ventricles, they depolarize and contract.

myocardial

Thus the impulse transmitted to the ventricular myocardial cells causes contraction of the _____.

ventricles

NOTE: The QRS complex on the EKG represents the beginning of ventricular contraction. The physical act of ventricular contraction actually lasts longer than the QRS complex, but we will consider the QRS complex to represent ventricular contraction. So the QRS complex represents depolarization of the ventricles, which causes ventricular contraction. Still with me?

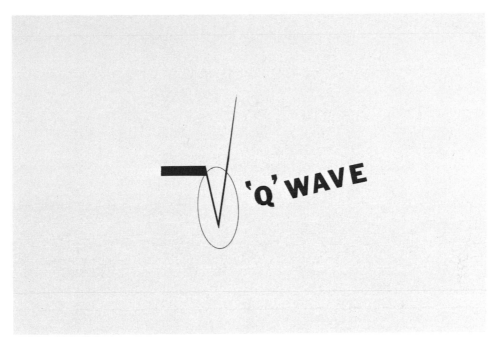

The Q wave is the first downward stroke of the QRS complex and it is followed by the upward R wave. The Q wave is often not present.

The Q wave is a wave which moves _____ on the   downward
tracing.

The Q wave, when present, occurs at the _____ of   beginning
the QRS complex and is the first downward deflection
of the complex.

The downward Q wave is followed by an upward ____ wave.   R

NOTE: If there is any upward deflection in a QRS complex
that appears before a "Q" wave, it is not a Q wave, for by
definition the Q wave is the first wave of the QRS complex.
The Q wave is always the first wave in the complex when
it is present.

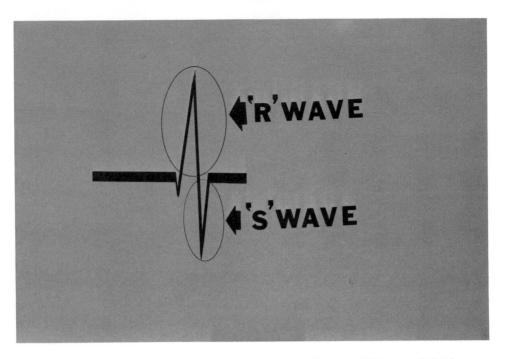

The upward R wave is followed by a downward S wave. This total QRS complex represents the electrical activity of ventricular contraction.

The first upward deflection of the QRS complex is the __ _____.

R wave

Any downward stroke PRECEDED by an upward stroke is an __ _____.

S wave

The complete QRS complex can be said to represent _____ depolarization (and the initiation of ventricular contraction).

ventricular

NOTE: The upward deflection is always called an R wave. Distinguishing the downward Q and S waves really depends on whether the downward wave occurs before or after the R wave. The Q occurs before the R wave and the S wave is after the R.

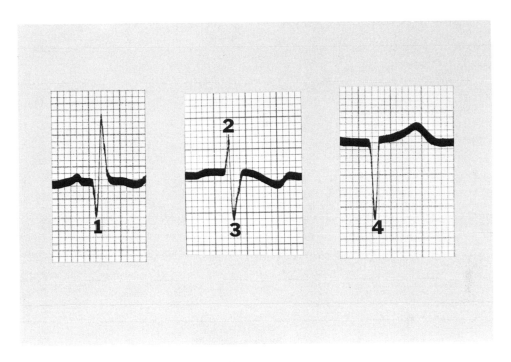

Name each of the above numbered waves.

1. _____.   Q

2. _____.   R

3. _____.   S

4. _____.   QS

NOTE: Number 4 was a little unfair. Because there is no
upward wave, we cannot determine whether number 4 is a Q
wave or an S. Therefore it is called, appropriately, a QS
wave and is considered to be a Q wave when we look for Q's.

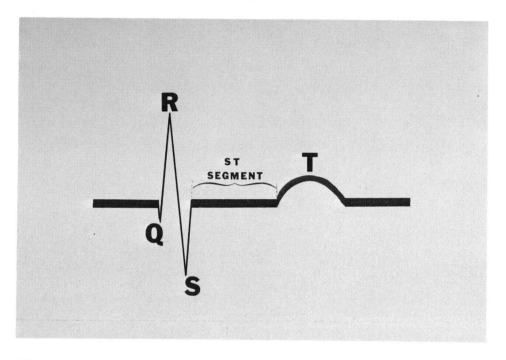

There is a pause after the QRS complex, then a T wave appears.

There is a _____ after the QRS complex.   pause

This pause is the _____ _____.   ST segment

NOTE: This ST segment which is merely the flat piece of
baseline between the QRS complex and the T wave is pretty
darn important as you will soon see.

The _____ _____ follows the pause.   T wave

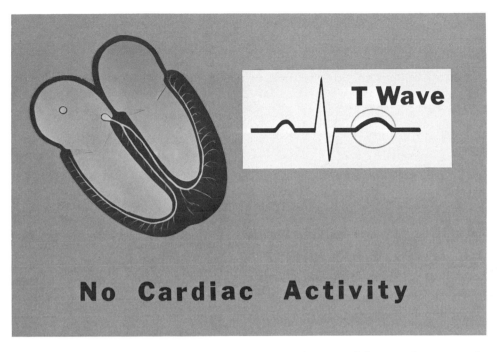

No Cardiac Activity

The T wave represents the repolarization of the ventricles so they may be stimulated again.

The T wave represents ventricular _____.

repolarization

Repolarization occurs so that the heart cells can regain the negative charge within each _____ so they can be depolarized again.

cell

NOTE: The ventricles have no physical response to repolarization. This is strictly an electrical phenomenon recorded on EKG. The atria also have a repolarization wave which is very small and usually lost within the QRS complex and therefore not seen ordinarily.

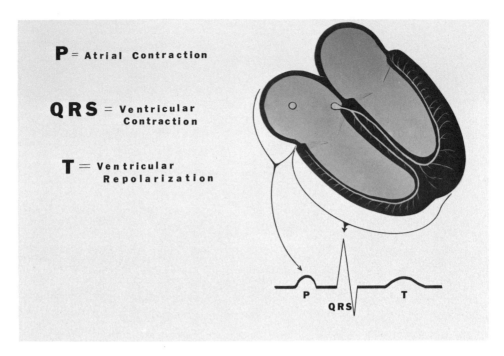

One cardiac cycle is represented by the P wave, QRS complex, and T wave. This cycle is repeated continuously.

The _____ wave represents atrial depolarization.   P

The _____ _____ represents ventricular depolarization.   QRS complex

The _____ wave represents ventricular repolarization.   T

NOTE: Physiologically a cardiac cycle represents atrial systole, ventricular systole (ventricular contraction), and the resting stage between beats.

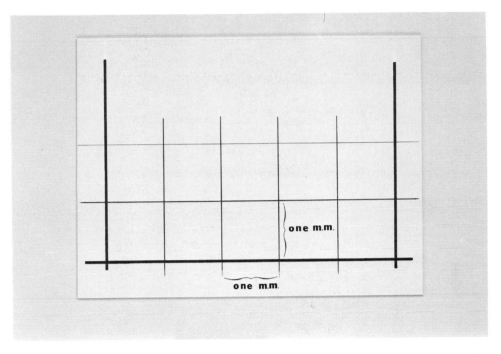

The EKG is recorded on ruled paper. The smallest divisions are one millimeter squares.

The electrocardiogram is recorded on a long strip of
_____ paper.

ruled (or graph)

The smallest divisions are _____ _____ long
and _____ _____ high.

one millimeter
one millimeter

There are _____ small squares between the heavy
black lines.

five

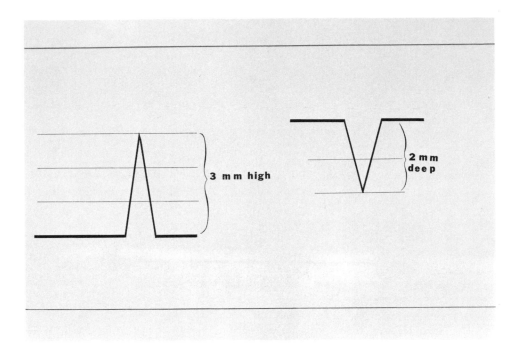

The height and depth of a wave is measured in millimeters and represents a measure of voltage.

The height or depth of waves may be measured in
_____.   millimeters

The height and depth of waves is a measure of _____.   voltage

The elevation or depression of segments of baseline is
similarly _____ in millimeters just like we measure   measured
waves.

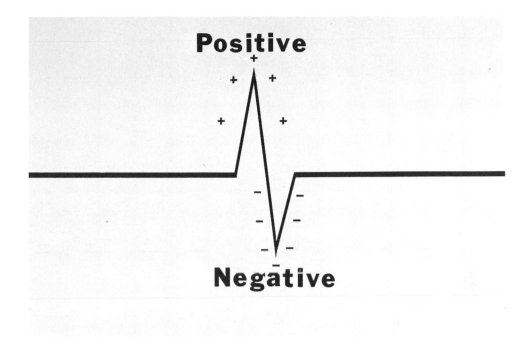

Upward deflections are called "positive" deflections. Downward deflections are called "negative" deflections on EKG's.

Positive deflections are _____ on the EKG.   upward

Negative deflections are _____ on the EKG.   downward

NOTE: When a wave of stimulation (depolarization) advances toward a positive electrode (skin electrode) this produces a positive (upward) deflection on EKG. You will recall that depolarization is an advancing wave of positive charge within the cells. So the advancing wave of positive charge in depolarization creates a positive deflection on EKG when this wave is moving toward a positive skin sensor. Be Positive! (If you're still a little shakey on this point return to page 7 for a second.)

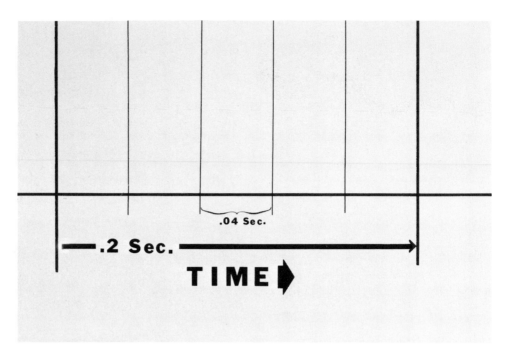

The horizontal axis represents time.

The amount of time represented by the distance between the heavy black lines is _____.

.2 seconds

There are _____ small squares between the heavy black lines.

five

Each small division (when measured horizontally between the fine lines) represents _____.

.04 seconds

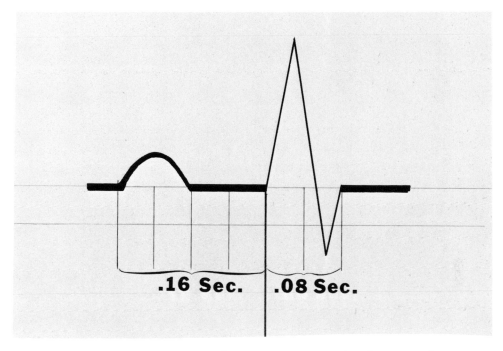

.16 Sec. | **.08 Sec.**

By measuring along the horizontal axis, we can find the duration of any part of the cardiac cycle.

The duration of any wave may be determined by measuring along the horizontal _____.

axis

Four of the fine divisions represents _____ seconds.

.16
(this is 16/100 seconds)

The amount of graph paper which passes under a point in .12 seconds is _____ small squares. (You don't have to be a mathematician to read EKG's.)

three

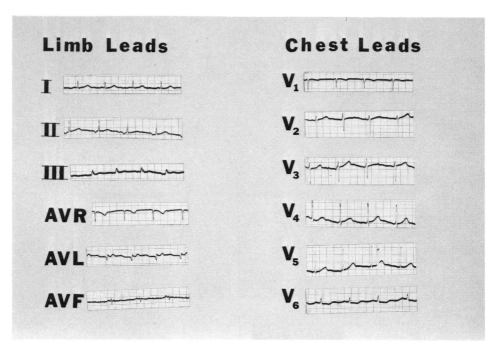

The standard EKG is composed of 12 separate leads.

The standard EKG is composed of six _____ leads and   chest
six _____ leads.   limb

NOTE: Leads not considered "standard" can be monitored
from various locations on the body.

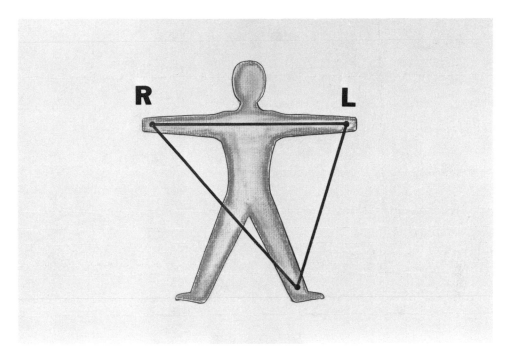

To obtain the limb leads, electrodes are placed on the right and left arms and the left leg forming a triangle (Einthoven's).

By placing electrodes on the right and left arms and left leg we can obtain the _____ leads.

limb

The placement of these electrodes forms a _____.

triangle

NOTE: The electrocardiogram was historically monitored by using these three locations for the electrode sensors.

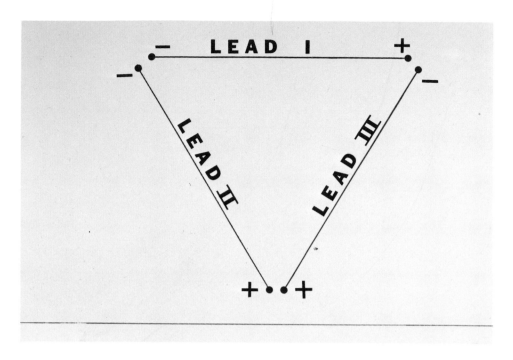

Each side of the triangle formed by the three electrodes, represents a lead (I, II, III) using different electrode pairs for each lead.

A pair of electrodes forms a _____.

lead

When considering a pair of electrodes, one is positive and one is _____.

negative

Lead I is horizontal and the left arm sensor is _____ while the right arm sensor is _____.

positive
negative

NOTE: The engineering wonders of the EKG machine permit us to make any skin sensor positive or negative depending on which lead the machine is monitoring.

When considering lead III, the left arm sensor is now _____ and the left leg sensor is _____.

negative
positive

NOTE: In reality, an electrode sensor is placed on the right leg as well for EKG monitoring. This helps stabilize the tracing.

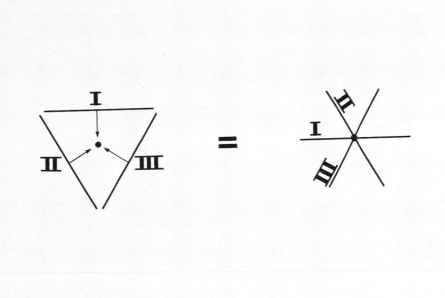

By pushing these three leads to the center of the triangle, there are three intersecting lines of reference.

The triangle has a center and each _____ may be moved to that center point.

    lead

By pushing leads I, II, and III to the center of the triangle, three intersecting lines of _____ are formed.

    reference

Although the leads are moved to the _____ of the triangle, they remain at the same angle.
(It's still the same leads yielding the same information.)

    center

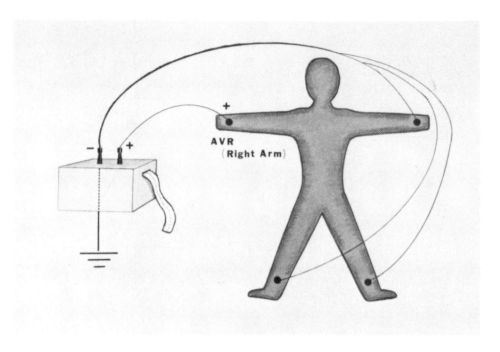

Another lead is the AVR lead. The AVR lead uses the right arm as positive and all other limb electrodes as a (common) ground (negative).*

The AVR lead uses the _____ _____ as positive.

right arm

All the other sensors are channeled into a common
_____.

ground

This "ground" is considered _____.
(positive or negative)

negative

NOTE: A man by the name of Frank Wilson discovered that in order to monitor a lead in this manner he had to amplify (augment) the voltage in the EKG machine to get a tracing of the same magnitude as leads I, II, and III. He named the lead A (augmented) V (voltage) R (Right arm), and he also created two more leads using the same technique.

* In reality the right foot sensor is never connected within the EKG machine while monitoring the "Augmented" leads.

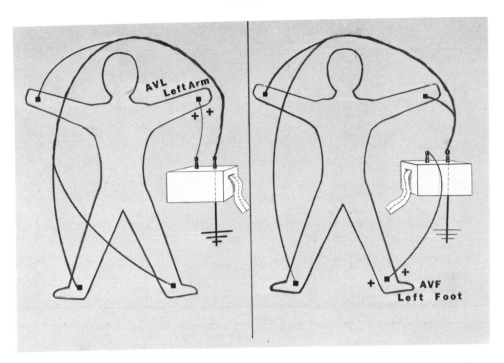

The remaining two limb leads are AVL and AVF and are obtained in a similar manner.

The AVL lead uses the left arm as _____.   positive

The other limb sensors in AVL are then channeled into a
ground and are considered _____.   negative

The positive sensor in AVF is on the _____ _____.   left foot

NOTE: AV*R* — Right arm positive
       AV*L* — Left arm positive
       AV*F* — Foot (left foot) positive

31

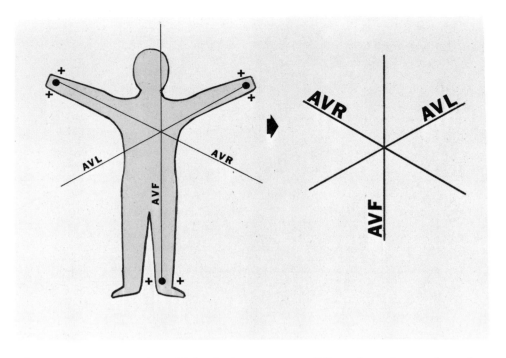

The AVR, AVL, and AVF leads intersect at different angles and produce three other intersecting lines of reference.

AVR, AVL, and AVF are also _____ leads.   limb

These leads _____ at 60 degree angles as do leads   intersect
I, II, and III.

Leads AVR, AVL, and AVF intersect at _____   angles
different from leads I, II, and III (and they split the angles
formed by I, II, III).

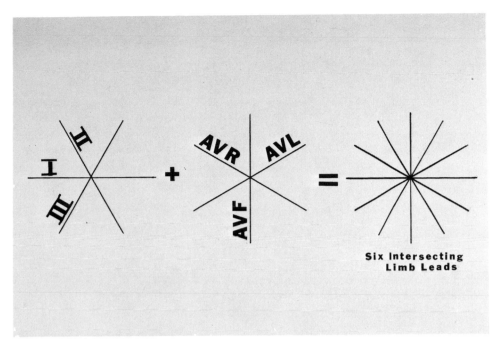

Six Intersecting
Limb Leads

All six leads, I, II, III, AVR, AVL, and AVF, meet to form six neatly inter-secting reference lines which lie in a flat plane on the patient's chest.

The six limb leads are I, II, III, _____,
_____, and _____.

AVR
AVL, AVF

If the intersecting leads I, II, and III, are superimposed over leads AVR, AVL, and AVF, we have _____ neatly intersecting leads (one every 30 degrees).

six

These limb leads may be visualized as lying in the
_____ _____ over the patient's chest.

flat plane

NOTE: This flat plane which can be visualized over the patient's chest is known as the *frontal* plane, if anyone asks you.

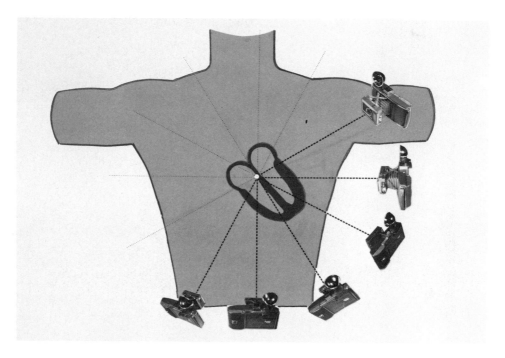

Each limb lead records from a different angle, thus each lead (I, II, III, AVR, AVL, and AVF) is a different view of the same cardiac activity.

The EKG records the same cardiac _____ in each lead.

activity

The waves look different in the various leads because this electrical activity is monitored from different _____.

positions

NOTE: Remember that the electrical activity never changes, but the electrode pairs are different for each lead, so the tracing changes slightly in each lead as we change the angle from which we monitor the cardiac activity. Keep in mind the fact that the wave of depolarization is a progressive wave of POSITIVE charges passing down the interior of the myocardial cells. If the depolarization moves toward a POSITIVE electrode sensor, this describes a POSITIVE (upward) deflection on the tracing for that particular lead. (A little repetitious, but this point should be stressed.)

It is important for you to visualize these intersecting leads. Why? Can you identify this car?

NOTE: This page sure seems empty doesn't it?

NOTE: Automobile experts are encouraged not to recognize the car for the sake of understanding the analogy.

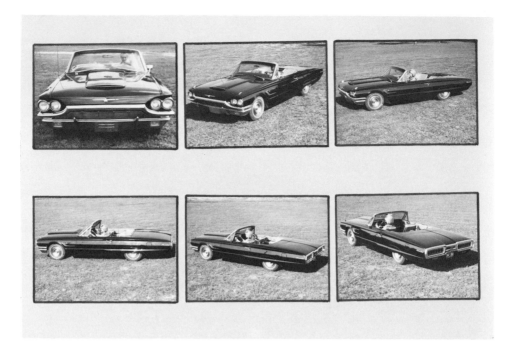

If you observe this same object from six different reference points, you will recognize the car.

NOTE: Observation from six angles is better than one. Thus monitoring cardiac electrical activity from six different angles gives us a much greater perspective. At this point you may take a sip of coffee and relax. Enjoy the automobile display before proceeding. The car, by the way, is a 1965 Thunderbird. The driver is not identified.

NOTE: You can't see the car's back bumper in the picture at top left. But with progressively different views you can tell more about the back bumper (or even the driver if you prefer). Similarly you may not be able to see a certain wave in a given lead, but with six different limb lead positions it should show up better in some leads.

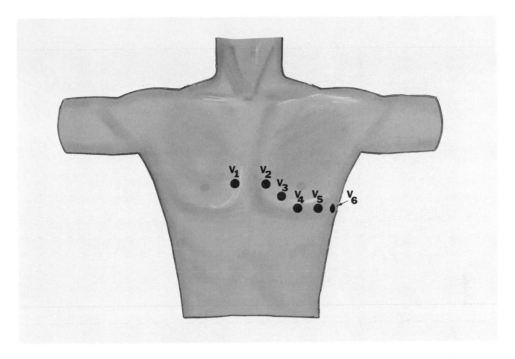

To obtain the six chest leads, a positive electrode is placed at six different positions around the chest.

The six chest leads are monitored from six progressively different positions on the _____.

chest

In all of the chest leads, the electrode sensor placed on the chest is considered _____. (This electrode is a suction cup which is moved to a different position on the chest for each different chest lead.)

positive

The chest leads numbered from V_1 to V_6 move in successive steps from the patient's _____ to his _____ side. Notice how the chest leads cover the heart in its anatomical position within the chest.

right
left

NOTE: Because the electrode sensor for the chest leads is always POSITIVE, a depolarization wave moving toward this sensor describes a POSITIVE or upward deflection on the tracing.

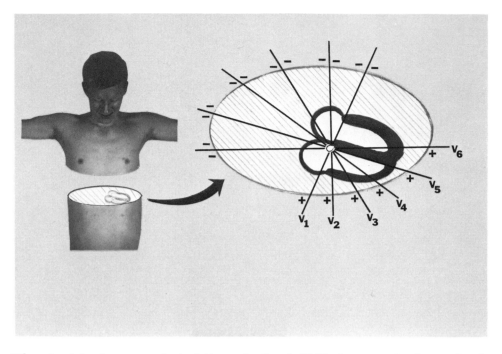

The chest leads are projected through the A V Node towards the patient's back which is the negative end of each chest lead.

The chest leads are considered _____ (positive or negative) posteriorly.

negative

If leads V_1 to V_6 are assumed to be the spokes of a wheel, the center of the wheel is the _____.

A V Node

Lead V_2 describes a straight line from the front to the _____ of the patient. The patient's back is negative in V_2.

back

NOTE: This plane which cuts the body into top and bottom halves is called the *horizontal* plane.

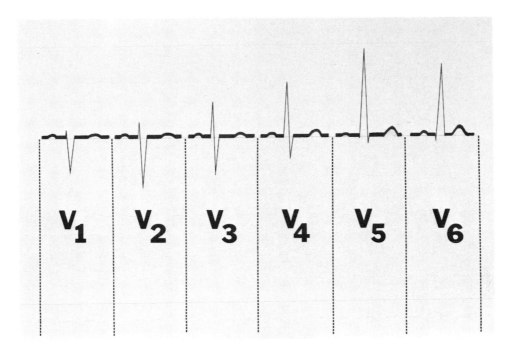

The EKG tracing will thus show progressive changes from V_1 to V_6.

The _____ tracing from V_1 to V_6 shows gradual changes in all the waves (as the position of each lead changes).

EKG

The QRS complex is mainly _____ (positive or negative) in lead V_1 normally (i.e. mainly above or below baseline).

negative

The QRS complex is mainly _____ (positive or negative) in lead V_6.

positive

This means that the (positive) wave of ventricular depolarization (represented by the QRS complex) is moving _____ (toward or away from) the POSITIVE chest electrode of lead V_6. (Make certain that you understand this concept. If not, check page 7.)

toward

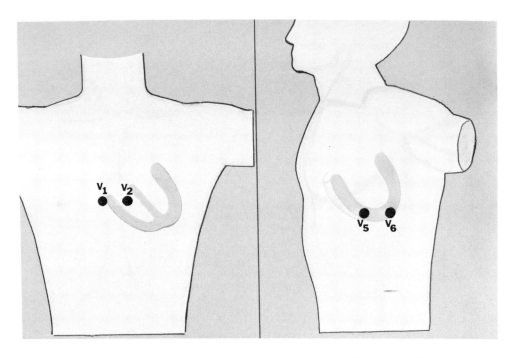

Leads V_1 and V_2 are placed over the right side of the heart, while V_5 and V_6 are over the left side of the heart.

Leads V_1 and V_2 are called the _____ chest leads.   right

The two leads over the left side of the heart are
_____ and _____ (and are called the left chest leads). V_5 and V_6

A depolarization wave moving toward the (positive)
chest electrode in lead V_6 will cause an _____   upward
deflection on the tracing.   (or positive)

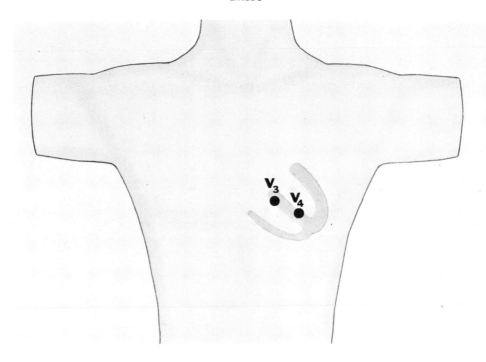

Leads V$_3$ and V$_4$ are located over the interventricular septum.

Leads V$_3$ and V$_4$ are located generally over the interventricular _____.

septum

NOTE: The interventricular septum is a common wall shared by the Right and Left Ventricle. In this area the A V Bundle divides into Right and Left Bundle Branches.

Considering lead V$_3$, the chest electrode is said to be _____. (positive or negative)

positive

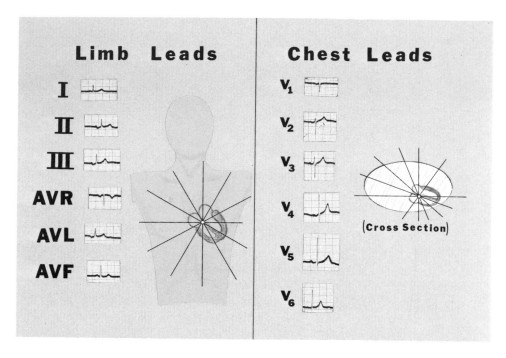

On a standard EKG mounting, the six chest leads and six limb leads are placed in a column. This is a 12 lead electrocardiogram.

The standard EKG has six chest leads usually mounted in progressive order from V_1 to _____.

V_6

The limb leads all lie in a plane which can be _____ over the chest of the patient. (This is the frontal plane).

visualized

The chest leads progressively encircle the heart in a _____ plane.

horizontal

NOTE: The chest leads form a plane which cuts the body into top and bottom halves.

1. Rate

2. Rhythm

3. Axis

4. Hypertrophy

5. Infarction

In the actual reading of an EKG you must check five general areas.

The most valuable areas to be considered in EKG
interpretation are Rate, Rhythm, Axis, Hypertrophy,
and Infarction. All of these areas are equally important,
so there are no blanks to fill in here.

NOTE: These five aspects should be considered in the above
order.

Be familiar with the definition of each of these five areas.

Ready?

In reading an EKG you should first consider the rate.

NOTE: The sign in this picture is not informing the driver about the rate of his car. The man holding the sign is a physician who has been monitoring the driver's transmitted EKG. The sign is informing the driver about his heart rate (he's a little excited).

When observing an EKG you should first check the _____.

rate

The rate is read as cycles per _____.

minute

The S A Node normally sets the rate of the heart beat.

The cardiac rate is normally set by the ——————.   S A Node

The S A Node is in the posterior wall of the right ——————.   atrium

The S A Node is the normal cardiac pace ——————.   maker

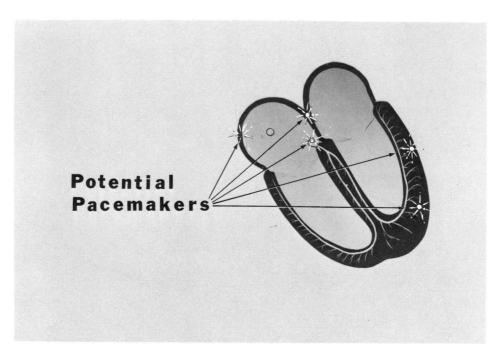

Potential Pacemakers

Other areas of the heart have the ability to set a pace if normal pacemaking mechanisms fail.

If the pacemaker does not function normally, there are _____ pacemakers available to take over the pace setting activity.

potential

NOTE: These potential pacemakers are often referred to as "ectopic" pacemakers. They generally function only in disease or emergency conditions.

The potential pacemakers are within all parts of the heart including the _____, ventricles, and A V Node.

atria

Under normal conditions these pacemakers are electrically quiet and do not _____. (That's why we call them "potential" pacemakers.)

function
(or operate
etc.)

Ectopic Atrial Pacemaker

Rate: 75/min

The atria have potential ectopic pacemakers, any one of which may take over pacemaking activity at a rate of about 75/minute.

If the S A Node fails, an ectopic atrial _____ may take over pacing activity.

pacemaker

When an atrial ectopic focus takes over the pacing responsibility, it usually discharges at a rate of ____/minute which is very close to the normal rate set by the S A Node.

75

NOTE: In emergency or pathological situations an ectopic atrial focus may suddenly begin to fire at a very fast rate of 150-250/minute.

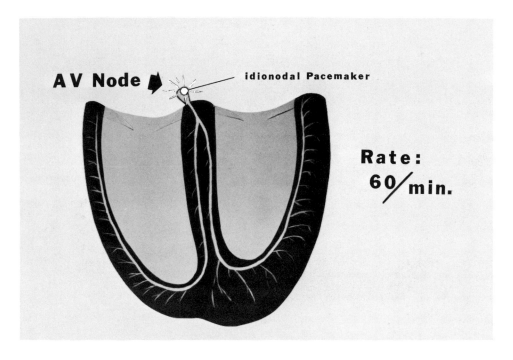

The A V Node sets a pace of 60 per minute if the usual stimulus from the atria is not present.

The A V _____ has potential pacemakers. Normally the A V Node is an electrical relay station which picks up the electrical stimulus of atrial depolarization and passes it on to the ventricles (i.e. down the Bundle Branch system).

Node

The usual rate set by an A V Node pacemaker (idionodal rate) is ____ per minute.

60

This ectopic pace is only begun if the normal stimulus fails to come down from the _____.

atria
(or S A Node
is more exact)

NOTE: Just like an atrial ectopic focus, a potential pacemaker in the A V Node may fire quite rapidly. It may suddenly begin discharging 150-250 times per minute in pathological or emergency situations.

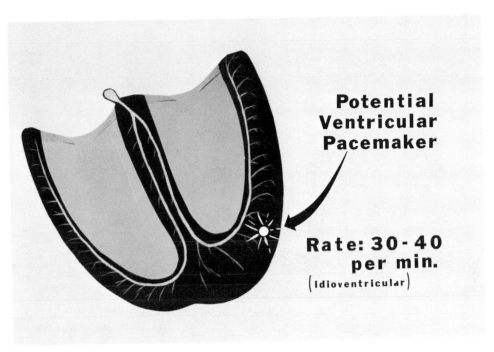

The ventricles also have potential pacemakers which set a rate of 30 to 40/minute if the normal stimulus from above is not present.

The _____ also have potential pacemakers.   ventricles

A ventricular pacemaker sets a pace of ____   30
to ____/minute when the normal stimulus from above   40
is absent.

This independent ventricular rate when present is called
an _____ rate.   idioventricular

NOTE: In emergencies when these pacemakers are subject
to poor blood supply (and low oxygen supply) they may fire
at very fast rates in attempt to correct the physiological
deficit. A ventricular ectopic focus may suddenly fire at a
rate of 150-250/minute under such conditions.

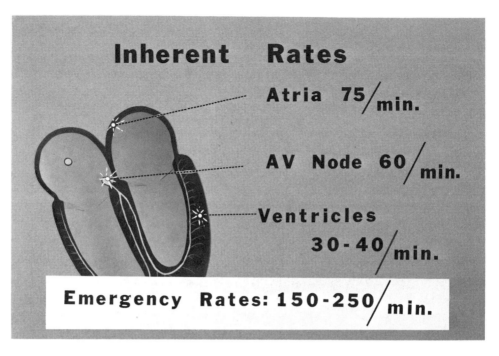

Inherent Rates

Atria 75/min.

AV Node 60/min.

Ventricles 30-40/min.

Emergency Rates: 150-250/min.

Ectopic foci in the atria, A V Node, and ventricles can discharge at their own inherent rate when normal pacemaking fails.

The ventricles can be paced by an ectopic focus at a rate of ____ to ____ per minute.

30 to 40

An atrial ectopic focus can pace the heart at a rate of ____ per minute, but a focus in the A V Node will pace at a slower rate of 60/minute.

75

NOTE: In emergency or pathological conditions the ectopic foci in any of these three areas may discharge at a rapid rate. The rapid rate (150 to 250/min.) is the same for the atrial, A V Node, and ventricular foci.

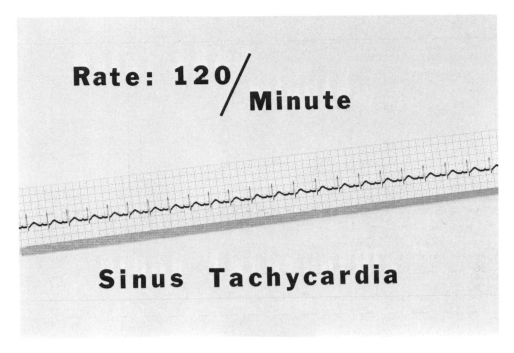

A rate of greater than 100/minute (with a normal rhythm) is called Sinus Tachycardia.

A rapid rate, with a normal _____, when greater than 100 per minute is a Sinus Tachycardia.   rhythm

By normal rhythm we mean a regular rhythm which proceeds normally from the _____, and each repeated   S A Node
cycle takes the same amount of time giving a steady continuous rate.

Sinus Tachycardia means the tachycardia _____   originates
in the Sino-Atrial Node (S A Node).   (begins)

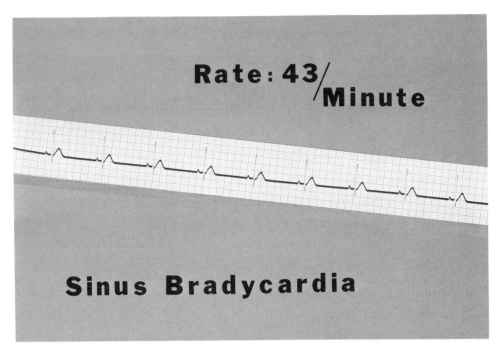

Rate: 43/Minute

Sinus Bradycardia

A rate of less than 60 per minute (with a normal rhythm) is called Sinus Bradycardia.

Sinus _____ means a very slow rate originating in the S A Node.

Bradycardia

A rate of less than _____ per minute indicates Sinus Bradycardia when a normal rhythm exists.

60

NOTE: Although the complexes are widely separated, the P, QRS, and T waves are still close together. There are merely longer pauses between cycles.

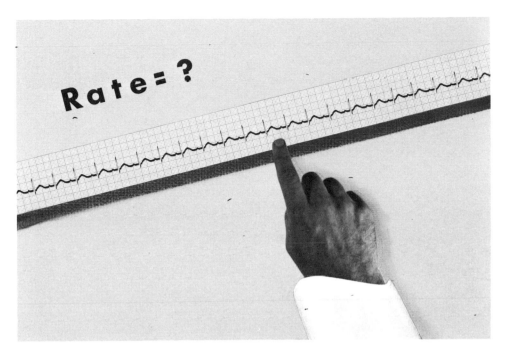

Our main objective is to rapidly note the rate without special devices.

When finishing this course you will be able to determine
the _____ rapidly.   rate

No special devices or rulers are necessary to _____   calculate
rate.

NOTE: In emergency situations you will probably not be
able to find your calculator. *THROW IT AWAY!*

Observation alone can tell us the _____.   rate

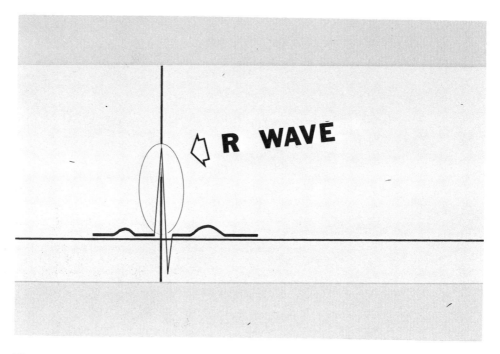

First: find a specific R wave that falls on a heavy black line.

To calculate rate you should first look at the _____ waves.   R

Now find one which peaks on a heavy black _____.   line

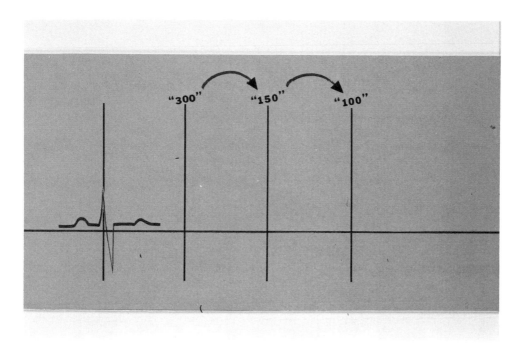

Next: Count off "300, 150, 100" for each heavy black line that follows, naming each one as shown. Memorize these numbers.

The next heavy black line is called "_____" ... followed
by "_____, _____" for the following heavy lines.

300
150, 100

NOTE: The line which the R wave peaks upon has no name.
We only name the lines that follow.

The three lines following the line where the R wave falls are
named "_____, _____, _____," in succession.

300, 150, 100

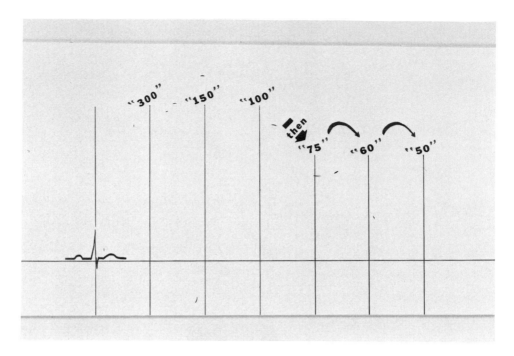

Then: Count off the next three lines after "300, 150, 100" as "75, 60, 50".

The next three lines after "300, 150, 100" are called
"_____, 60, and 50".

75

Remember the next three lines together as "_____,
_____, _____".

75
60, 50

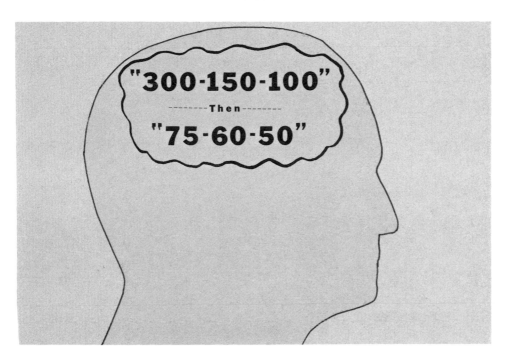

Now: Memorize these triplicates until they are second nature. Make certain you can say the triplicates without using the picture.

These triplicates, "300, 150, 100" and "75, 60, 50"
must be _____.   memorized

Be able to name the lines following that one on which an
R wave _____, but it is easier to remember them as   peaks
triplicates.

Do not count the following lines — *name* them with
the _____.   triplicates

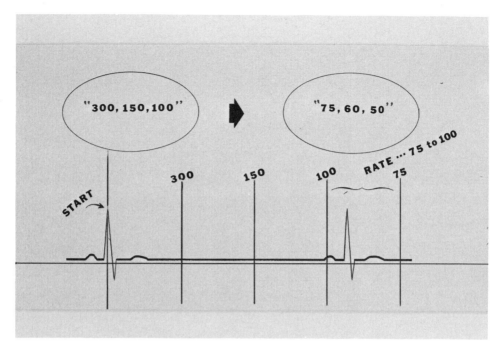

Where the next R wave falls determines the rate. It is that simple.

The first R wave peaked upon a heavy line, now look
for the next _____ _____.   R wave

Where the next R wave falls gives the _____. There is no   rate
mathematical computation necessary.

If the R wave falls on "75" the rate is 75 per _____.   minute

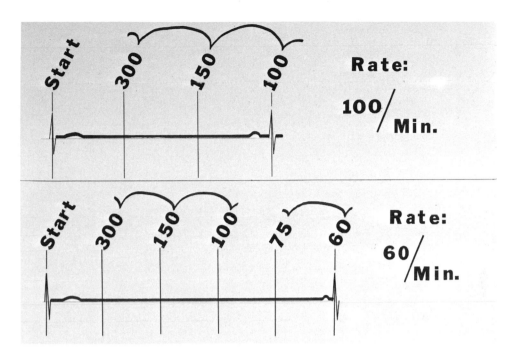

Knowing the triplicates "300, 150, 100" and "75, 60, 50", you can merely look at an EKG and tell the approximate rate.

The triplicates are: first "_____, _____, _____."
                  then "_____, _____, _____."

300, 150, 100
75, 60, 50

If the second R wave falls between "100" and "75", this is probably a normal _____. (Remember that normal pulse rate is about 80.)

rate

By merely remembering the _____, you can immediately tell the rate.

triplicates

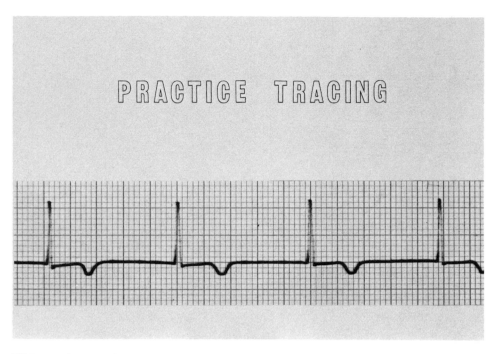

This is the EKG tracing from a patient with a heart rate slower than his usual rate.

The rate in the above tracing is _____ cycles per minute.   60

If you were told that this rate originated from an ectopic pacemaker, you would probably suspect the _____   A V Node
(by rate alone).

NOTE: This is indeed a rhythm originating in the A V Node and that is why you can't see any P waves.

You no longer need to depend on a slide calculator. Now you may determine the rate very easily by simple observation.

You can determine the rate on an EKG tracing at any time by _____ alone.

observation

Do not depend on an EKG ruler or slide calculator to determine _____.

rate

You may need to know the rate on an _____ tracing when you don't have your ruler in your pocket.

EKG

NOTE: You will always have your brain with you (until that time when brain transplants are done and you may have someone else's brain).

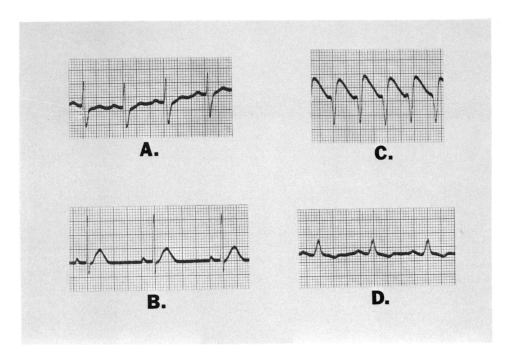

Give the approximate rates of the above EKG tracings.

A. _____   100

B. _____   60

C. _____   150 or so

D. _____   75

The distance between the heavy black lines represents 1/300 min.

So two 1/300 min. units = 2/300 min. = 1/150 min. (or 150/min. rate)

and three 1/300 units = 3/300 = 1/100 min. (or 100/min. rate)

There is a logical explanation for the seemingly unusual rate denominations for the heavy black lines.

The number of time units between five consecutive heavy
black lines is _____.   4

So this represents 4/300 minute or a rate of _____   75
per minute.

Therefore if a heart contracts 75 times/minute, we would
expect _____ QRS complexes within a span of five heavy   one
black lines.

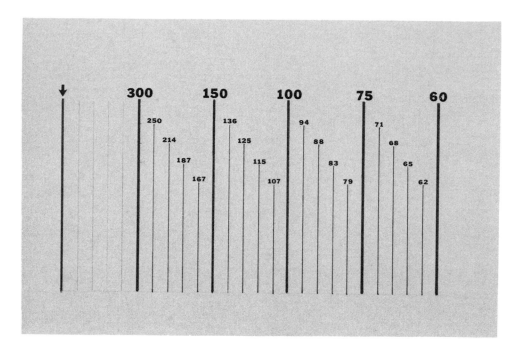

Although memorization of the fine divisions is a tremendous undertaking, more exact calculation of rates is possible.

NOTE: It is admittedly a great task to memorize the fine subdivisions, but it is convenient to have this information here for your reference should you need it.

NOTE: For rates less than sixty see the next few pages for simplified methods of calculation.

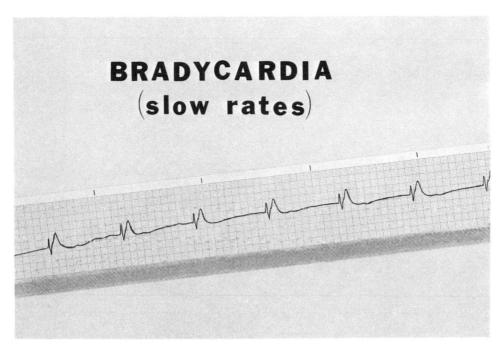

BRADYCARDIA
(slow rates)

For very slow rates we offer another easy method for recognizing the rate rapidly.

Slow rates are called _____.   Bradycardia

For these very slow rates you can use another method
to _____ them.   calculate

NOTE: The triplicates give us a very large range of rates.
"300, 150, 100" and "75, 60, 50" means that you can
determine rates from 300 to 50. Very slow rates infer a
rate less than 60 per minute.

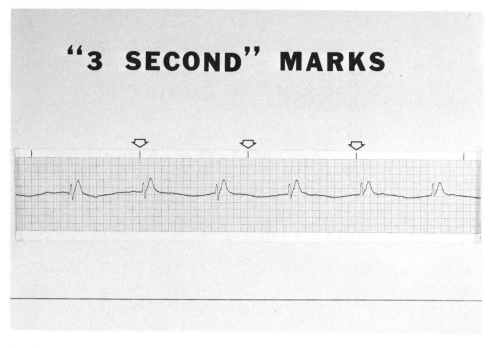

"3 SECOND" MARKS

At the top of the EKG tracing there are small vertical marks which note "three second" intervals.

There are small _____ marks above the graph portion of the EKG tracing. Find a strip of EKG tracing and examine it.

vertical

These vertical marks are called the "three second" _____ marks.

interval

NOTE: Some EKG paper has 3 second intervals marked with a block dot.

When the EKG machine is running, the length of paper between two of these vertical marks passes under the stylus needle in _____ _____.

three seconds

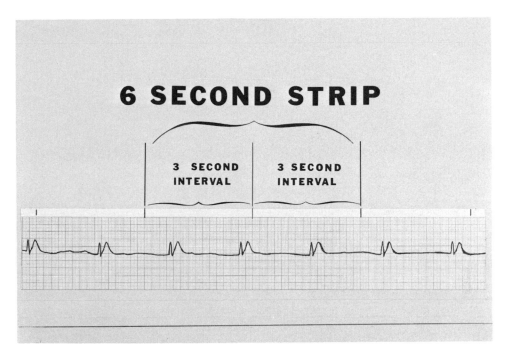

Taking two of the three second intervals, we have a 6 second strip.

A three second interval is noted as the distance
between two of the _____ marks.

vertical
(or three second
marks)

Taking two of the three second intervals gives us
a _____ second strip.

six

This six second strip represents the amount of
_____ used by the machine in six seconds.

paper

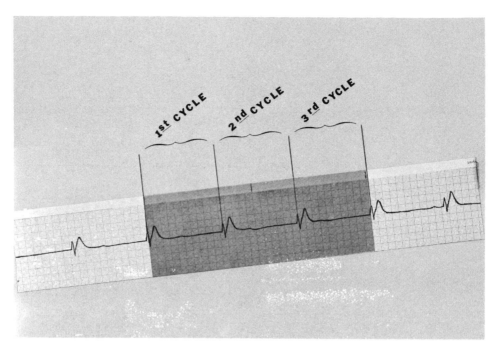

Count the number of complete cycles (R wave to R wave is one cycle) in this strip. With very slow rates there will be few cycles.

A complete cardiac _____ is counted from a specific wave until the wave is repeated again.

cycle

So, R wave to _____ wave gives one cycle.

R

Count the number of cycles in the six second _____.

strip

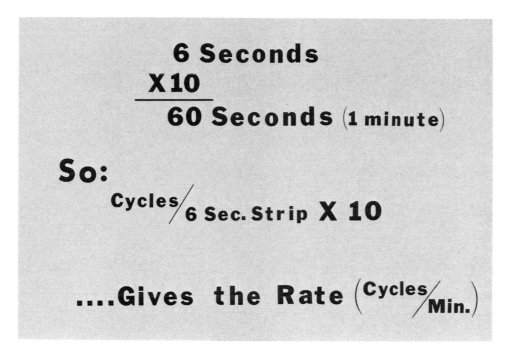

$$\frac{6 \text{ Seconds}}{60 \text{ Seconds}} \times 10 \quad (1 \text{ minute})$$

So:

$$\text{Cycles}/\text{6 Sec. Strip} \times 10$$

....Gives the Rate $\left(\text{Cycles}/\text{Min.}\right)$

The rate is obtained by multiplying the number of cycles in the six second strip by 10.

Ten of the 6 second strips equal one _____ (time)   minute
recorded on EKG.

The number of cycles per minute is the _____.   rate

So cycles per six second strip multiplied by
_____ equals the rate.   ten

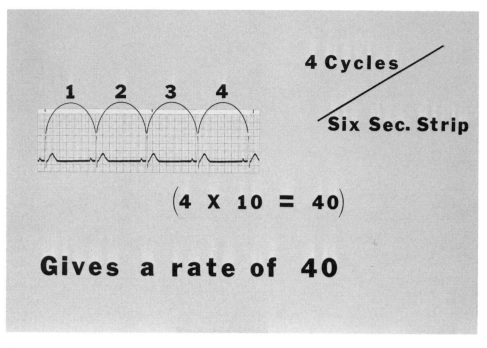

Place a zero on the right of the number of cycles/six second strip and you have the rate.

For very slow rates or _____ first find a   bradycardia
six second strip.

.... count the number of _____ in this strip.   cycles

.... and multiply by _____ to get the rate.   ten

NOTE: Multiplying by ten may be done by placing a zero
on the right side of the number of cycles per six second strip.
For instance 5 cycles (per six second strip) gives a rate of 50.

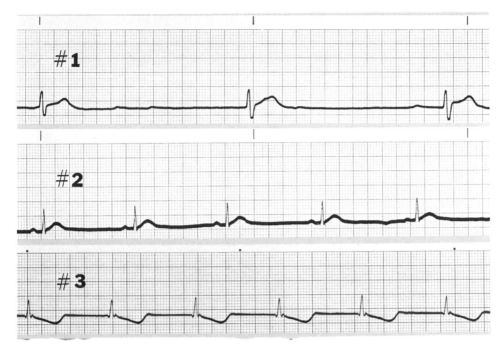

Give the approximate rates of these EKG's.

Rates: No. 1 _____ per minute   20
       No. 2 _____ per minute   45
       No. 3 _____ per minute   50

NOTE: Obtain some EKG tracings and amaze yourself at
how easily you can now determine the rate.

NOTE: Review Rate by turning to the small notebook
sheets at the end of this book (page 269).

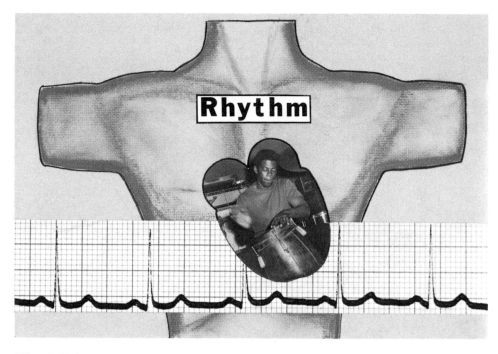

The EKG provides the most accurate means for identifying cardiac arrhythmias (abnormal rhythms) which can be easily diagnosed by knowing the electro-physiology of the heart.

_____ literally means without rhythm, however we use it to denote abnormal rhythm, or breaks in the regularity of a normal rhythm.

Arrhythmia

The _____ records all the electrical phenomena of the heart which may not be seen, felt, or heard on physical examination, and therefore provides a very accurate means for determining rhythm changes.

EKG

NOTE: To understand the arrhythmias you must first be familiar with the normal electro-physiology of the heart (i.e. the normal pathway of electrical conduction).

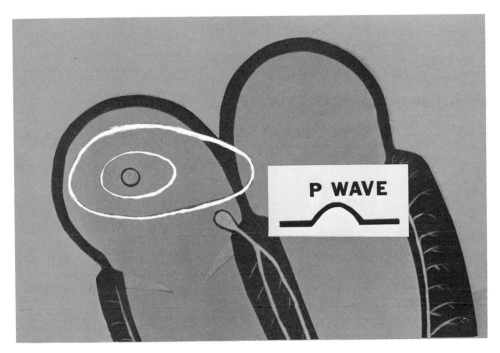

The pacemaker impulse from the S A Node spreads through both atria as a wave of depolarization.

It is the _____ which initiates the stimulus for pacemaking activity.

S A Node

The S A Node sends out regular impulses which cause the atria to _____.

contract

This wave of stimulation called _____ spreads out from the S A Node in wave fashion and describes a P wave on the EKG.

depolarization

NOTE: The S A Node is really the "Sino-Atrial" node, so impulses originating from this node are often called by the stem "Sinus" or "Sino" — as in Regular "Sinus" Rhythm.

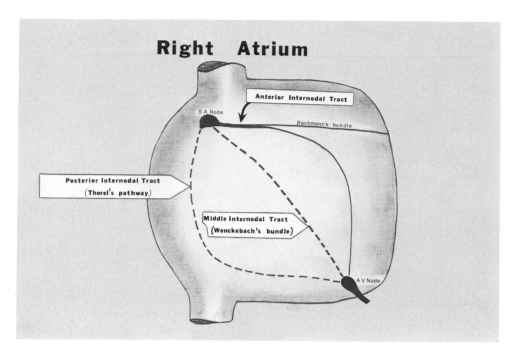

The atrial conduction system consists of three specialized conduction pathways.

Three general atrial conduction pathways are known today; the anterior, middle, and _____ internodal tracts.

posterior

The posterior internodal tract is known as _____ pathway.

Thorel's

This page serves as a reference; for specific pathological conditions involving these preferential conduction pathways have not as yet been described, but certainly will in the future. For now, it suffices to recognize their existance.

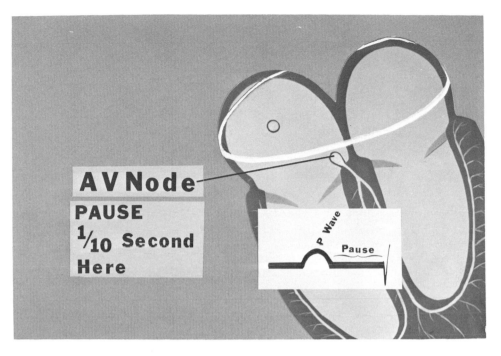

As this electrical impulse reaches the A V Node, there is a 1/10 second pause before the A V Node is stimulated.

As the impulse of atrial depolarization reaches the A V Node
there is a _____.   pause

NOTE: The A V Node is named for its position between
the Atria and the Ventricles (thus "A V"). Unfortunately
the shorthand notation for the A V Node is simply "Nodal".
"Nodal rhythms" or "Nodal premature beats" therefore
refer to the A V Node.

This pause during which there is no cardiac electrical
activity is merely represented by the flat piece of baseline
between the _____ wave and the QRS complex.   P

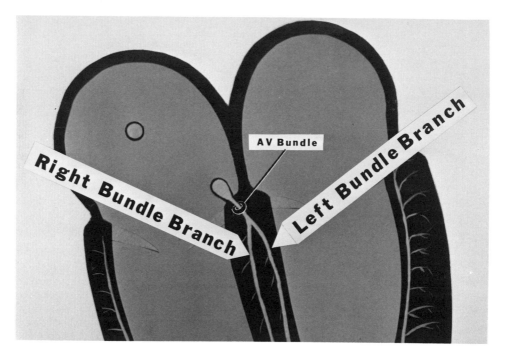

Once stimulated the A V Node transmits the electrical stimulus down the Right and Left Bundle Branches to stimulate both ventricles.

Once the A V Node is stimulated it transmits the electrical impulse to the A V _____.

Bundle

From the A V Bundle the impulse is conducted down the Left and Right Bundle _____.

Branches

The impulse quickly spreads to both _____ to initiate their simultaneous depolarization.

ventricles

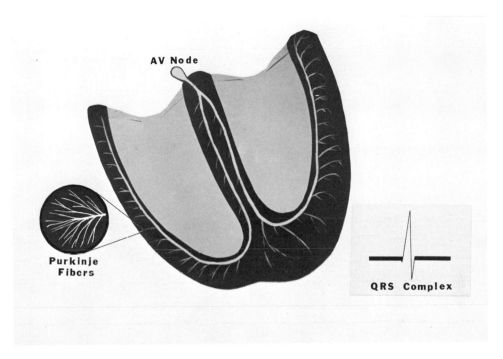

This A V Node-Bundle Branch system is made of specialized nervous tissue which carries the electrical stimulus (depolarization) rapidly.

The A V Node-Bundle Branch system is made of specialized _____ tissue.

nervous

This nervous tissue conducts electrical _____ rapidly.

impulses

NOTE: I would like to stress the fact that this specialized nervous tissue carries electrical impulses through the ventricles rapidly. Cardiac muscle itself conducts bio-electrical charges more slowly, therefore it is easy to recognize pathological impulses that originate outside the nervous conduction system of the ventricles (they are slower on EKG).

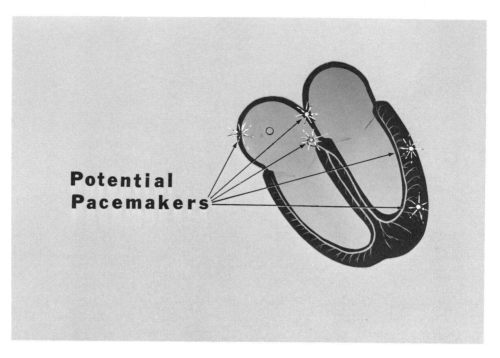

There are potential (ectopic) pacemakers in both atria, in the A V Node, and in both ventricles, which can take over if normal pacing fails.

Potential pacemakers exist in the atria, ventricles, and the _____.

A V Node

These are emergency pacemakers which can take over _____ activity if normal pacing activity fails.

pacing

Because these potential pacemakers do not usually function under normal physiological conditions, they are called _____ (abnormal location) foci. They may emit one or a series of stimuli which initiate depolarization in that area.

ectopic

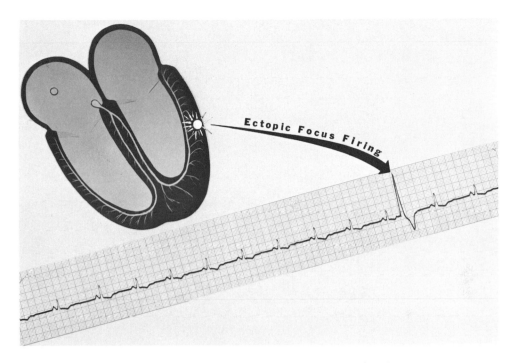

These ectopic foci occasionally emit an electrical impulse in non-emergency situations, especially in heart disease.

The ectopic focus is an area which can emit
electrical _____.

stimuli
(or impulses)

NOTE: Focus is singular, foci refers to more than one focus.

The presence of impulses from ectopic foci may indicate
heart _____.

disease

NOTE: All the arrhythmias may be easily understood simply by knowing the normal electro-physiology (conduction) of the heart and realizing the existence of ectopic foci. As each of the arrhythmias are presented, visualize what is taking place in the heart (electrically) and the interpretation of the tracing becomes an easy matter. Do not memorize patterns. Lasting knowledge results from understanding.

These ectopic foci may send out one or a _____ of
electrical impulses.

series

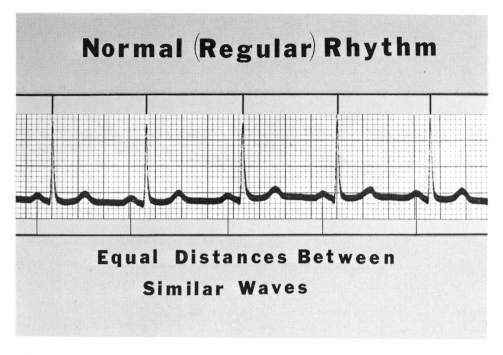

Normal (Regular) Rhythm

Equal Distances Between Similar Waves

The normal cardiac rhythm is such that there is a constant distance between similar waves.

The normal rhythm of the heart is said to be _____.

regular

The distance between similar _____ is always the same in a classical regular rhythm.

waves

NOTE: The normal rhythm is often referred to as a Regular Sinus Rhythm or Normal Sinus Rhythm as it originates in the S A Node.

Rhythm

Varying Rhythm

Extra Beats and Skips

Rapid Rhythm

Heart Blocks

The arrhythmias may be broken down into large general categories.

NOTE: It is not necessary to memorize these four groups of arrhythmias. These classifications are general areas to help you rapidly recognize the pathology by appearance. By determining the physiological equivalent of what appears on the tracing, you will be able to understand the mechanisms involved in all the arrhythmias.

Varying Rhythm

Sinus Arrhythmia

Wandering Pacemaker

Atrial Fibrillation

Varying rhythm is a category of irregular rhythms with a normal sequence (P — QRS — T) of waves, however the rhythm changes continuously.

The _____ rhythms are those rhythms which show general irregularity with no predictable pattern of recurrence.

varying

NOTE: Some people call these arrhythmias irregularly irregular since no regular pattern of irregularity can be found.

The normal sequence of waves (i.e. _____ — QRS — T) is usually seen in this classification.

P

However the interval between P — QRS — T cycle is constantly _____.

changing

Sinus Arrhythmia

·Varying rhythm

·P Waves identical

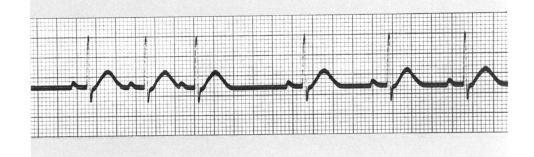

Sinus Arrhythmia is a varying irregular rhythm often due to coronary artery disease. (Sick S A Node disease)

In Sinus Arrhythmia the pacemaking impulses _____ in the S A Node (thus the prefix Sinus). Because all impulses originate in the S A Node, all _____ waves are identical.

originate

P

The pacemaking activity is quite irregular and the pacemaker's _____ are sent out at varying intervals.

impulses

The P — QRS — T waves of each cycle are usually _____ and similar in size and shape, but the timing of the cycles is irregular.

normal

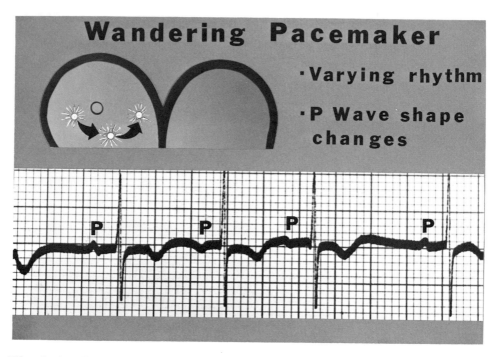

Wandering Pacemaker is a varying rhythm caused by changing position of the pacemaker. It is characterized by P waves of varying shape.

In Wandering Pacemaker the pacemaking _____ wanders from focus to focus.

activity

The resulting rhythm is very _____ and there is no consistent pattern of rhythm.

irregular

The ___ waves of Wandering Pacemaker are of various shapes as the pacemaking activity changes location.

P

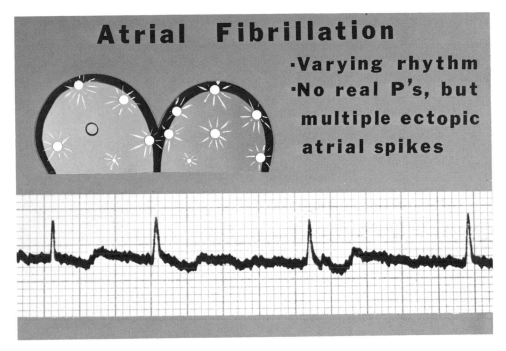

Atrial Fibrillation is caused by the firing of multiple foci in the atria. No single impulse depolarizes the atria completely and only an occasional impulse gets through to the A V Node.

Atrial Fibrillation is caused by multiple ectopic _____ in the atria which constantly emit electrical impulses.

foci

Since no single impulse depolarizes both atria, we cannot find any real _____ waves.

P

This is always a totally irregular rhythm since only random impulses get to the A V Node to initiate a _____ complex. The irregular ventricular responses may produce a rapid or slow rhythm.

QRS

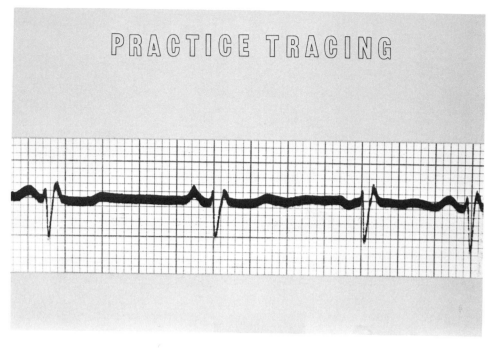

PRACTICE TRACING

This tracing was monitored from a patient with a very irregular pulse.

In this practice tracing we notice an irregular rhythm in
which we can see discernable _____ waves, so we can rule out
Atrial Fibrillation.

P

The P waves are not identical, so we can say that this tracing
is probably not _____ Arrhythmia.

Sinus

Our diagnosis is therefore _____.
Easy, isn't it!

Wandering
Pacemaker

Extra Beats and Skips

Premature Beats

Escape Beats

Sinus Arrest

Extra beats may be recognized as waves which appear earlier than expected. Skips refer to blank areas of baseline.

NOTE: Extra Beats and Skips is a general classification given to a group of arrhythmias which can be recognized by sight. By scanning the tracing, the break in the repeating continuity of cycles is easily spotted. Further identification is necessary to explain why the pause or extra beat is present.

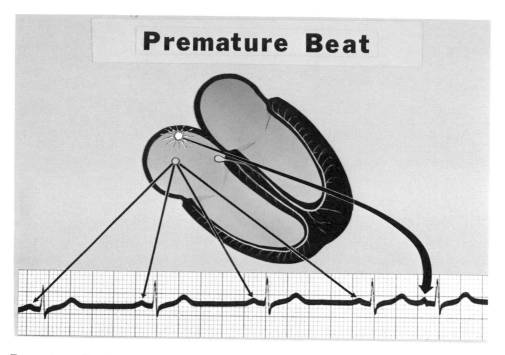

Premature Beat

Premature Beats are caused by a premature firing of various ectopic foci creating waves which appear earlier than usual in the cycle. (The first four cycles here are normal.)

Premature beats like premature babies appear _____ than expected.

earlier

These premature beats generally originate from _____ foci.

ectopic

They may be normal looking _____ or bizarre forms, but they all appear suddenly, very early in the cycle.

waves

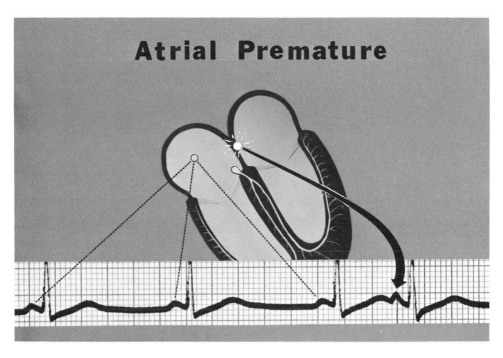

Atrial Premature

Premature atrial stimulation from an atrial ectopic focus produces an abnormal P wave earlier than expected.

A premature atrial beat originates in an ectopic focus in
an atrium and appears much earlier than the normal
_____ wave should.   P

Because this impulse does not originate in the _____,
it will not appear like the other P waves in the same lead.   S A Node

This ectopic impulse depolarizes the atria in a manner similar
to the normal impulse, so the A V Node picks up and
transmits the impulse just as if it were a normal _____ wave.   P

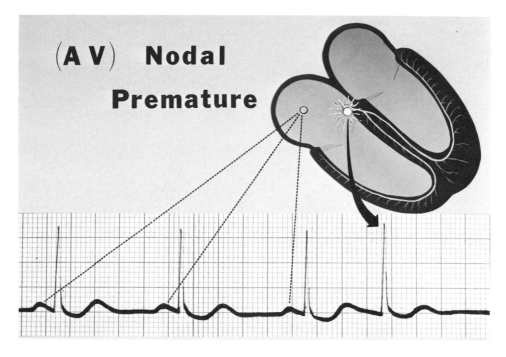

Premature nodal stimulation originates from an ectopic discharge in the A V Node, so the impulse proceeds down the Bundle Branch pathway in the normal manner.

Nodal Premature stimulation originates in a focus in the A V Node which fires before the _____ begins a normal cycle.

S A Node

Therefore one usually notices a normal appearing _____ which occurs very early and is generally not preceded by a P wave.

QRS

NOTE: Occasionally this Nodal focus will send an impulse upward to stimulate the atria from below (RETROGRADE CONDUCTION). When it occurs, this backwards atrial depolarization may create an inverted P wave which can appear just before or after the QRS, or this peculiar inverted P wave may be mixed in with the QRS complex.

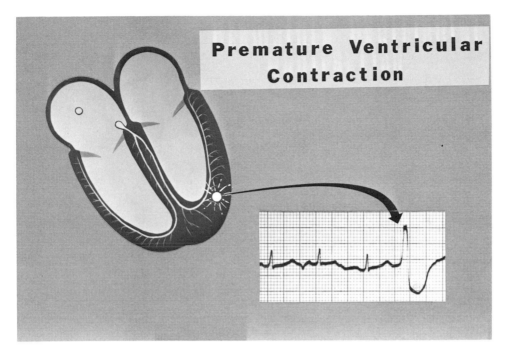

Premature Ventricular Contraction

Premature Ventricular Contractions (P.V.C.'s) originate from an ectopic focus in a ventricle.

An ectopic focus may originate an impulse from somewhere in one of the _____.

ventricles

The ventricular ectopic beat like all other premature beats occurs very early in the cycle (before a _____ wave is expected).

P

The resultant Premature Ventricular Contraction commonly known as a _____ is easily recognized on the electrocardiogram tracing.

P.V.C.

NOTE: P.V.C. denotes a ventricular "contraction". When you see a P.V.C., remember that there is a (premature) ventricular contraction and an associated pulse beat just like that produced by a normal QRS.

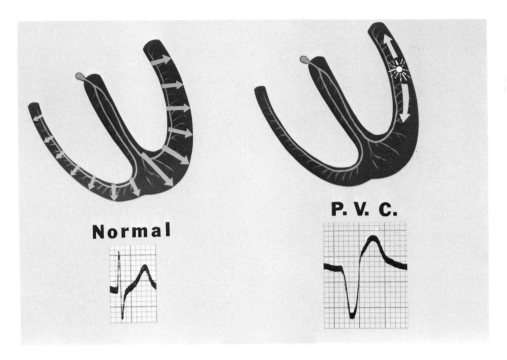

Normal

P. V. C.

The impulse of the P.V.C. does not follow the usual Bundle Branch conduction system, therefore conduction is slow (very wide QRS).

The Bundle Branch system conducts the normal electrical stimulus of ventricular depolarization very rapidly yielding a narrow QRS _____.

complex (wave is a wrong answer because there are three waves)

However the impulse of the P.V.C. originates in the myocardium (outside the nervous conduction system), and the myocardial cells conduct the impulse very _____.

slowly

NOTE: The nervous conduction system of the heart transmits impulses at a rate of 2-4 meters/second. Normal myocardium transmits electrical impulses at a rate of only one meter/second (without the aid of the nervous conduction system). Therefore the nervous conduction system of the ventricles transmits electrical impulses 2 to 4 times faster than the muscle tissue (myocardium) can alone.

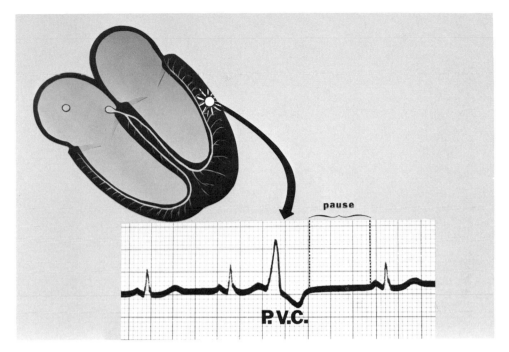

There is a long (compensatory) pause after the P.V.C.

There is a compensatory pause after a _____ during
which the heart is electrically silent.

P.V.C.

NOTE: During normal ventricular conduction, the left and
right ventricles depolarize simultaneously. As a result,
depolarization going toward the left (left ventricle) is
somewhat opposed by depolarization going toward the right
(right ventricle) and a relatively small (normal) QRS
results. But a P.V.C. originates in one ventricle which
therefore depolarizes before the other. So the deflections from
a P.V.C. are very tall and very deep (no simultaneous
opposing depolarization from opposite sides) on the
electrocardiogram. P.V.C.'s have greater deflections than
normal QRS complexes.

NOTE: _Interpolated beats_ are P.V.C.'s that are somehow
sandwiched between the normal beats of a tracing, producing
no compensatory pause and no disturbance in the normal
regular rhythm.

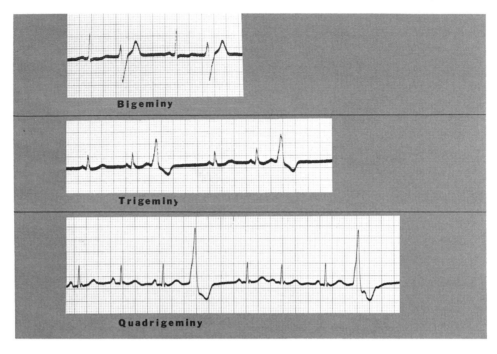

Bigeminy

Trigeminy

Quadrigeminy

P.V.C.'s may become coupled with one or more normal beats to produce Bigeminy, Trigeminy, etc.

P.V.C.'s occasionally become _____ with one or more normal cycles, and this pattern recurs over and over.

coupled

When a P.V.C. becomes coupled with a normal beat, this is called _____ as this pattern recurs with each normal beat.

Bigeminy

If you were to see a P.V.C. apparently coupled with two normal beats, and the pattern repeated itself many times, one could call this runs of _____.

Trigeminy

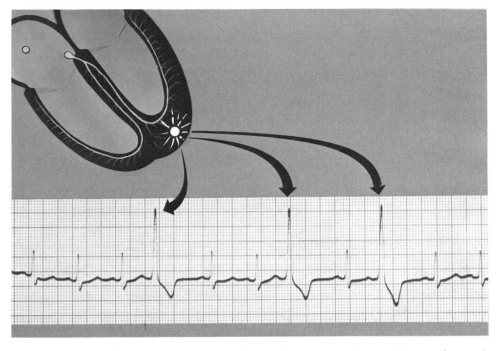

Numerous P.V.C.'s may originate from the same focus. More than six P.V.C.'s per minute is considered pathological.

While monitoring a given lead you may notice a P.V.C. appearing quite often, but it always looks the same. Because each P.V.C. is identical, we can assume that they all _____ from the same focus.

originated

P.V.C.'s often indicate that the heart's own (coronary) blood supply is poor, so their appearance alerts us that something may be wrong. _____ P.V.C.'s per minute is pathological.

Six

NOTE: In cases where the coronary blood flow is adequate but the blood is poorly oxygenated (e.g. drowning, pulmonary pathology, tracheal obstruction etc.) the heart recognizes poor oxygenation (and high CO_2) and ventricular ectopic foci will discharge frequently.

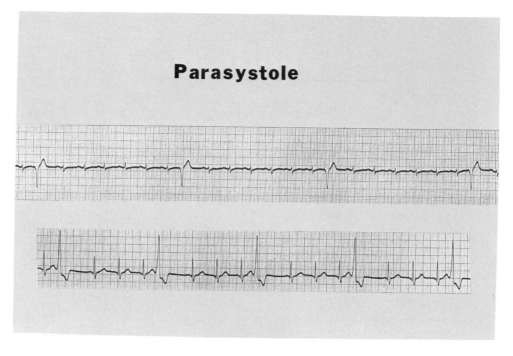

Parasystole

Parasystole is a dual rhythm caused by two pacemakers one of which is ectopic and generally ventricular in origin.

Ventricular ectopic rhythms produce P.V.C-like QRS complexes, are generally slow, and when associated with another (supraventricular) rhythm are known as _____.   parasystole

NOTE: The ventricular ectopic beats demonstrate a regular rhythmicity in parasystole, and due to a "protective" phenomenon very few beats are dropped (non-conducted) from the refractoriness of the supraventricular rhythm.

When one recognizes _____ that are "coupled" with   P.V.C.'s
a long series of normal beats you should suspect parasystole.

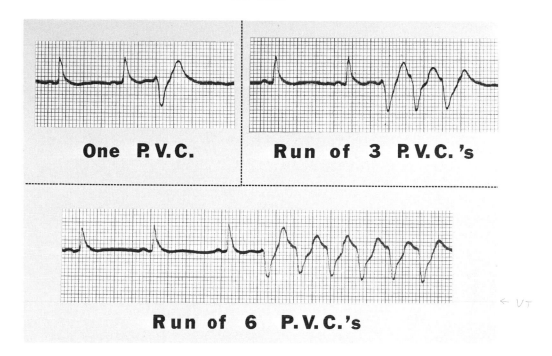

One P.V.C.   **Run of 3 P.V.C.'s**

Run of 6 P.V.C.'s

A single ventricular ectopic focus may fire once, or it may fire a series of successive impulses to produce a run of P.V.C.'s.

A single _____ ectopic focus may fire a series of   ventricular
discharges in rapid succession.

Runs of P.V.C.'s are probably more serious than occasional
single P.V.C.'s from a single _____.   focus

NOTE: A run of more than four P.V.C.'s in rapid succession
is called a run of Ventricular Tachycardia (see the last
example in the above frame), but we will go deeper
into this later.

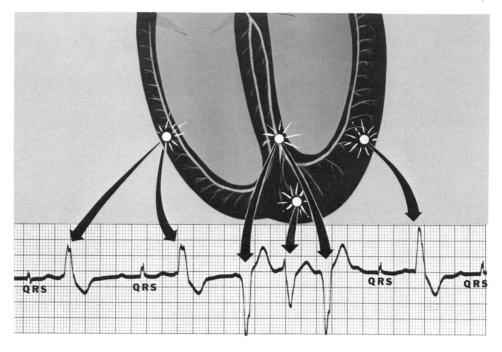

Multifocal P.V.C.'s are produced by multiple ventricular ectopic foci. Each focus produces an identical appearing P.V.C. every time it fires.

In a given lead the P.V.C.'s originating from the _____ focus will appear the same.

same

NOTE: The appearance of numerous multifocal P.V.C.'s is indeed dangerous and requires rapid treatment. Realizing that a single ventricular focus can take off and fire a series of discharges causing dangerous arrhythmias (e.g. Ventricular Tachycardia), the appearance of numerous *multifocal* P.V.C.'s means that there is trouble ahead, and the chance of developing a dangerous or even deadly arrhythmia (like Ventricular Fibrillation) is much enhanced.

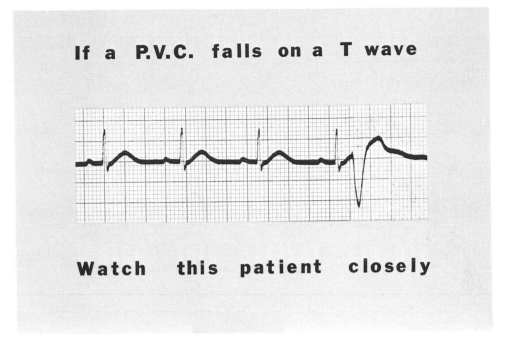

If a P.V.C. falls on a T wave, it occurs during a vulnerable period and dangerous arrhythmias may result.

P.V.C.'s ordinarily occur just after the _____ wave of a normal cycle.

T

When a P.V.C. falls on a T wave of a normal cycle, it is catching the ventricles during a _____ period.

vulnerable

A P.V.C. which falls on a T wave may cause the _____ ectopic focus which is involved to discharge repeatedly.

ventricular

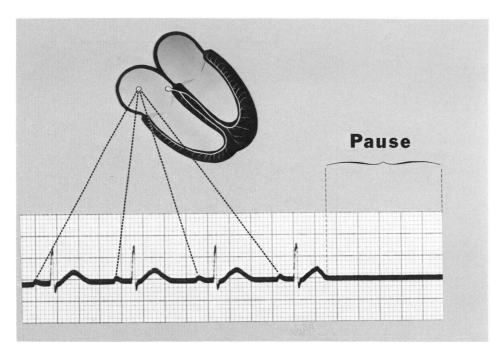

Escape Beats occur when the normal pacemaker fails to elicit a stimulus for one or more cycles, so an impatient ectopic focus fires.

When the _____ (S A Node) fails to fire its normal regular stimulus, the heart remains temporarily silent.

pacemaker

On the EKG tracing the failure of the pacemaker to fire is seen as a flat area of baseline which is free of _____.

waves

NOTE: One does not usually have to look for these skip areas. They are very obvious as they break the continuity of a regular rhythm on the tracing.

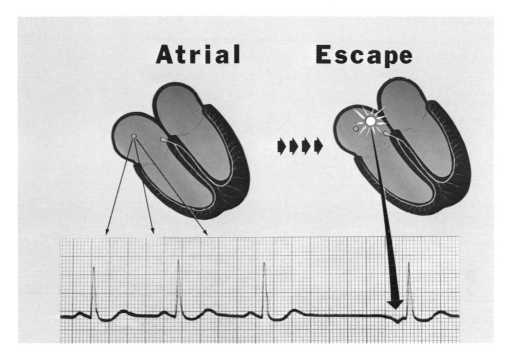

An ectopic focus in the atria may fire an impulse after such a pause, stimulating the atria. Conduction then proceeds down through the A V Node normally.

Because the other areas know that they must be
_____ regularly, they grow impatient when a pause   stimulated
of electrical silence appears.

An ectopic _____ then "escapes" to emit an electrical   focus
impulse of its own to stimulate the electrically quiet heart.

When an atrial ectopic focus discharges after a silent pause
of more than one cycle, we call this an Atrial _____   Escape
Beat, and because this P wave originates ectopically it does
not look like the other P waves.

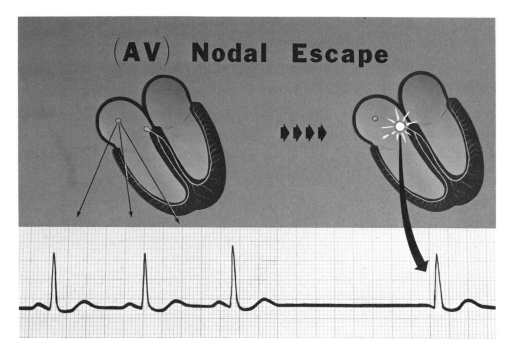

Nodal Escape Beats originate in the A V Node and stimulate the ventricles via the normal conduction system yielding a normal QRS after the pause.

Nodal Escape Beats occur after the S A Node fails to fire for at least one cycle, leaving the heart _____ silent.

electrically

The Nodal Escape Beat originates in the A V Node, and the impulse follows the usual nervous conduction system of the Left and Right _____ Branches.

Bundle

This produces a normal appearing QRS _____ because the ventricles are depolarized just as though the A V Node was stimulated from above (normally) by atrial depolarization.

complex

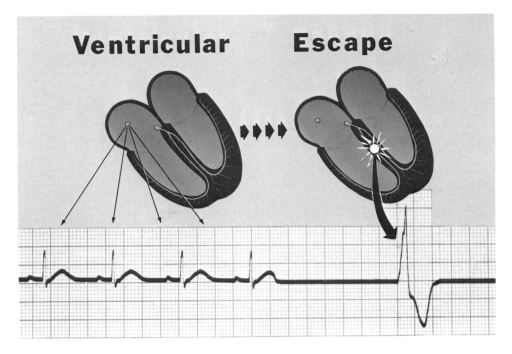

Ventricular Escape

Ventricular Escape Beats originate in an ectopic ventricular focus resulting in a P.V.C. type ventricular response after a pause in the rhythm.

Ventricular Escape Beats originate in a ventricular
_____ focus which fires an impulse because of the lack
of cardiac electrical activity from above.

ectopic

This ventricular ectopic response, because it originates from a ventricular ectopic focus, yields a _____ type complex after the pause.

P.V.C.

NOTE: Any time a ventricular ectopic focus discharges, a P.V.C. type complex appears as the ventricles depolarize.

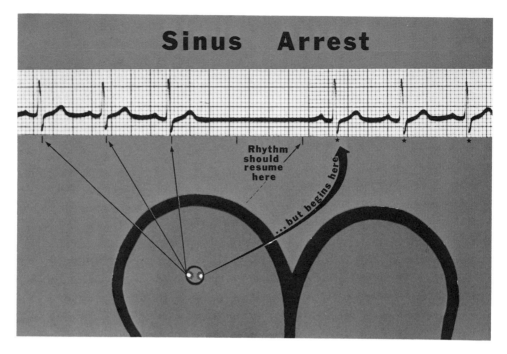

Sinus Arrest occurs when the S A Node's pacemaking area suddenly is "arrested" and does not send out pacemaking stimuli. After the pause of the Sinus Arrest another *new* pacemaking area takes over but it does not fall in step with the old rate.

Sinus Arrest refers to an arrest of the pacemaking activity of the _____, producing temporary electrical silence.

S A Node

Another pacer must resume pacemaking activity, so another area of the S A Node or a nearby ectopic atrial focus begins to fire to maintain a regular _____.

rhythm

NOTE: Because a new (ectopic) pacemaker takes over the responsibility of pacing, the new pacemaker sets its own new rate which is usually not in step with the rate of the arrested pacemaker.

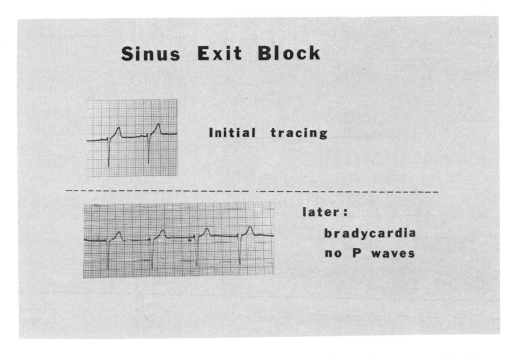

Occasionally there are patients who show no atrial activity due to a blockage (or non-existance) of S A Node pacing, i.e. the rhythmic discharge cannot progress beyond the S A Node.

When a tracing demonstrates no evidence of P waves in all leads and a bradycardia,_____ should be suspected.

sinus exit block

NOTE: Sinus exit block may require the implantation of an artificial pacemaker.

NOTE: Occasionally, patients with Sinus Exit Block have bursts of tachycardia.

NOTE: Sinus Arrest and Sinus Exit Block are essentially the same. Remember that the pacing responsibility can be taken over by a potential pacemaker in the atria, A.V. Node, or Ventricles (with associated rate and wave patterns seen with the respective new pacemaker).

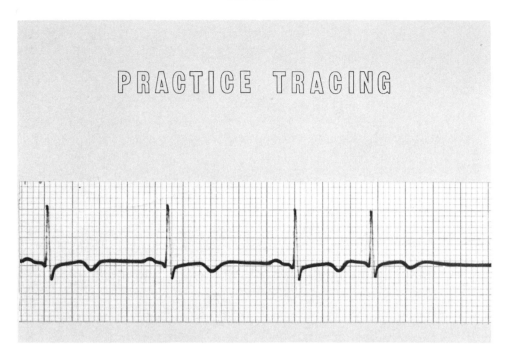

The discerning eye of a Coronary Care nurse detected a beat which appeared a little too early in an EKG strip taken from a patient's monitor.

By looking at the last QRS complex in the strip you discover that it is not preceded by a _____ wave.   P

The last QRS complex looks the same as the other QRS's, so we know that the last one followed the usual Bundle Branch _____ system.   conduction

The last ventricular depolarization on this strip probably originated in the _____ and it is a premature beat.   A V Node

Rapid Rhythms

Paroxysmal Tachycardia

Atrial Flutter

Ventricular Flutter

Atrial Fibrillation

Ventricular Fibrillation

Rapid rhythms may be regular or irregular but they all have some rapidly occurring phenomena.

NOTE: Rapid rhythms are easily recognized, but the differentiation of the varieties of tachycardia is essential. A knowledge where these rapid rhythms originate and how they are maintained is necessary for making a diagnosis. A basic understanding of normal conduction and the presence of potential ectopic pacemakers simplifies our diagnosis.

Paroxysmal (Sudden) Tachycardia

Paroxysmal Tachycardia means sudden rapid heart rate which usually arises from an ectopic pacemaker.

_____ means a rapid heart rate.

Tachycardia

Paroxysmal means _____.

sudden

Paroxysmal Tachycardia usually occurs spontaneously from an ectopic focus which fires impulses in _____ succession.

rapid

NOTE: The normal pacemaker, the S A Node, may increase the heart rate in certain conditions. This is called a "Sinus" Tachycardia since it originates in the Sino-atrial Node, and is often due to excitement, exercise, stimulating drugs, shock, etc.

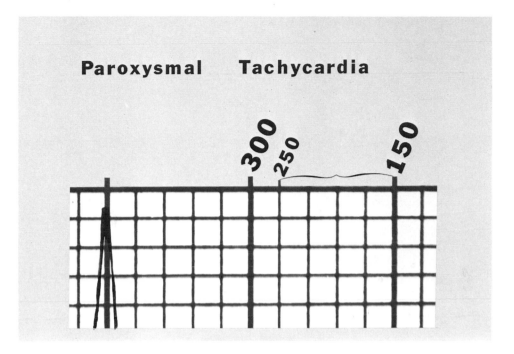

The range of the paroxysmal tachycardias is 150-250/minute. You should be able to quickly recognize them by observation.

When calculating rate, we find an R wave which peaks on a heavy black line. The next three heavy black lines are called "300, 150, _____".

100

The fine line just to the right of the line named "300" is 250. Therefore if an R wave falls on the first heavy black line (above illustration), the next R wave will fall within the bracketed area during paroxysmal _____.

tachycardia

Now you should be able to recognize a paroxysmal tachycardia by rapidly noting the rate range of _____ to 250.

150

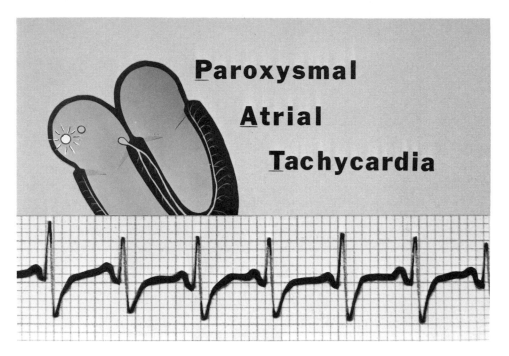

Paroxysmal Atrial Tachycardia is caused by the sudden rapid firing of an ectopic atrial pacemaker.

Paroxysmal Atrial Tachycardia is a _____ heart rate originating from an ectopic focus in one of the atria. The rate is usually about 150 to 250.

sudden

Because the focus is ectopic, the P waves in P.A.T. usually do not look like the other P waves (before the tachycardia) in the same _____.

lead

Each ectopic impulse stimulates the _____ and is conducted down the normal A V Node-Bundle Branch ventricular pathway yielding normal P — QRS — T cycles.

atria

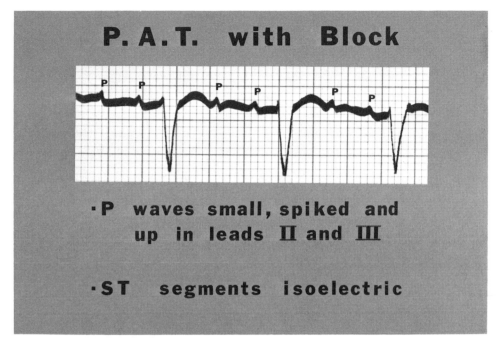

P. A. T. with Block

·P waves small, spiked and up in leads II and III

·ST segments isoelectric

In *Paroxysmal Atrial Tachycardia with block* there is more than one P to every QRS. This often signifies digitalis toxicity.

P.A.T. with block is recognized by the fact that each of the individual P waves does not have a QRS response, ie. one or more of the atrial impulses is blocked and does not get to the _____.

A V Node

So we may see two or more (spiked) P waves for each _____ but there is still an atrial tachycardia.

QRS

P.A.T. with block is often an indication of digitalis _____.

toxicity

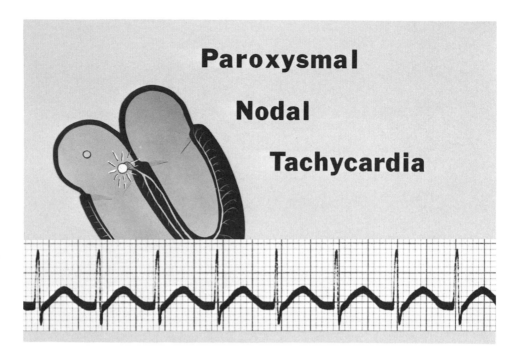

Paroxysmal Nodal Tachycardia is caused by an ectopic pacemaker in the A V Node.

Paroxysmal Nodal Tachycardia is a rapid pace (150-250) set by an ectopic focus in the _____.

A V Node

NOTE: As mentioned earlier, ectopic foci in the A V Node have a strange way of sometimes stimulating the atria from below by retrograde conduction. This may produce inverted P waves which can appear immediately before or just after each QRS complex in the tachycardia. If you are aware of this phenomenon, you will recognize it from time to time.

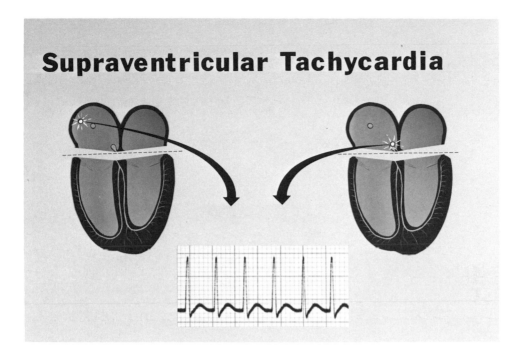

Supraventricular Tachycardia

Paroxysmal Atrial Tachycardia and Paroxysmal Nodal Tachycardia originate above the ventricles and are known as "Supraventricular Tachycardias".

Paroxysmal Atrial Tachycardia and Paroxysmal Nodal
Tachycardia both originate above the ventricles and
are known as _____ Tachycardias.

Supraventricular

NOTE: Paroxysmal Atrial Tachycardia may occur at
such a rapid rate that the P waves run into the preceding
T waves and appear like one wave. This makes the
differentiation of these two tachycardias very difficult;
however because they are both treated in the same manner,
differentiation of P.A.T. and P.N.T. is not essential.
So if we cannot make a distinction between the two, we
can just say Supraventricular Tachycardia.

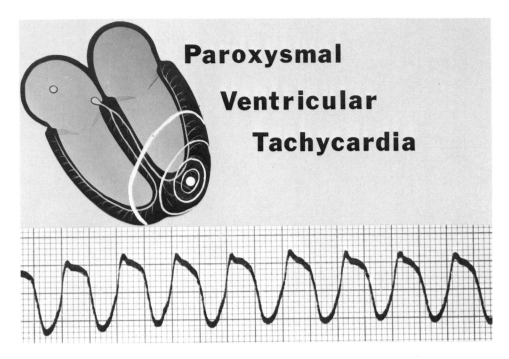

Paroxysmal *Ventricular Tachycardia* is initiated by a ventricular ectopic pacemaker. It has a characteristic pattern.

Paroxysmal Ventricular Tachycardia originates suddenly in an ectopic focus in one of the _____ producing a (ventricular) rate of 150-250.

ventricles

Sudden runs of Ventricular Tachycardia appear like a series or _____ of P.V.C.'s. (Which in reality it is.)

run

NOTE: Although the atria still depolarize regularly at their own inherent rate, distinct P waves are usually not seen.

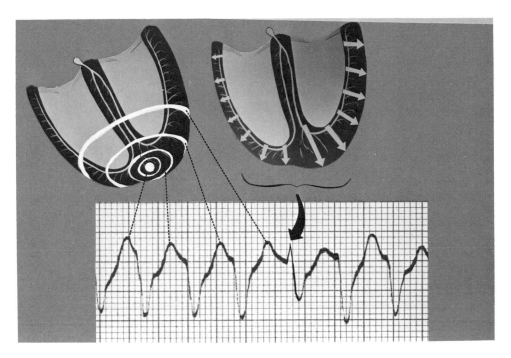

An occasional atrial impulse may break through from above to stimulate a normal appearing complex during Ventricular Tachycardia.

Occasionally one of the impulses from the regularly beating atria breaks through to _____ the A V Node.   stimulate

The A V Node is only vulnerable to a stimulus from above at certain times during Ventricular _____, so   Tachycardia only a few atrial impulses stimulate the A V Node.

NOTE: When the A V Node is stimulated by an atrial depolarization from above (during Ventricular Tachycardia), the impulse begins to follow the normal Bundle Branch pathway. A nearly normal looking QRS complex results (or at least the beginning of a QRS). This normal looking portion of a QRS usually fuses with a P.V.C. type complex from the ectopic focus creating a "Fusion Beat". Occasionally the impulse from above will be carried to completion to capture a normal QRS creating a "Capture Beat". The presence of "captures" or "fusions" cinches our diagnosis of Ventricular Tachycardia.

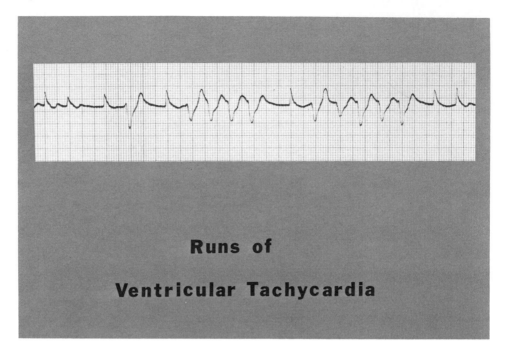

Runs of

Ventricular Tachycardia

Runs of Paroxysmal Ventricular Tachycardia may signify coronary artery disease.

Paroxysmal Ventricular Tachycardia appears like a run of _____.   P.V.C.'s

This is a pathological condition and usually signifies coronary _____ disease.   artery

NOTE: This rapid ventricular rate originates from a ventricular ectopic focus, and the rate is really too fast for the heart to function effectively, so it should be treated quickly.

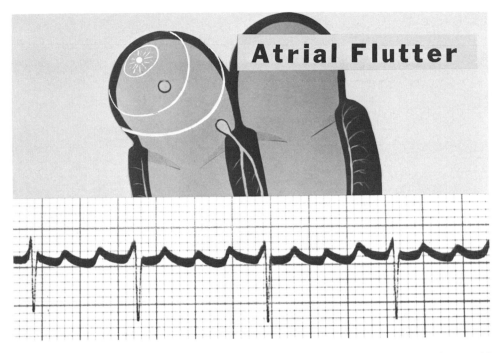

Atrial Flutter originates in an atrial ectopic focus. P waves occur in rapid succession and each is identical to the next.

In atrial flutter an ectopic focus in the atria fires at a rate of 250-350 to produce a rapid succession of _____ depolarizations.

atrial

Because there is only one ectopic _____ discharging, each "P wave" looks identical to all the others. The atrial depolarizations originate ectopically so they are not really P waves, and therefore are often called flutter waves.

focus

It is only the occasional atrial stimulus which will stimulate the A V Node, so there are a few flutter waves in series before a QRS _____ is seen.

complex

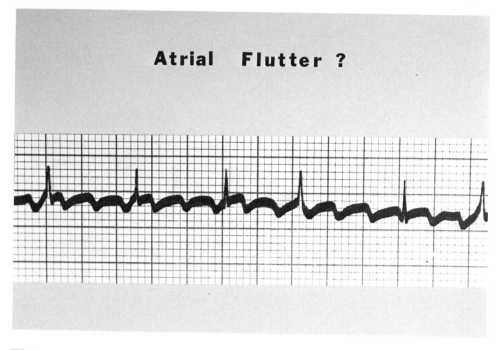

Atrial Flutter ?

This tracing looks somewhat like atrial flutter, but to make it more classical you have to turn it upside down.

When in doubt about atrial flutter, inverting the _____ tracing may be very helpful.

NOTE: Atrial flutter is characterized by a series of identical "P waves" in rapid succession or back-to-back flutter waves. Because the waves are identical, they are described as having the appearance of the teeth of a saw or "saw tooth" baseline. It is important to note that the waves fall in rapid succession and there is no flat baseline between them. Turn back to P.A.T. with block and make sure you understand the difference.

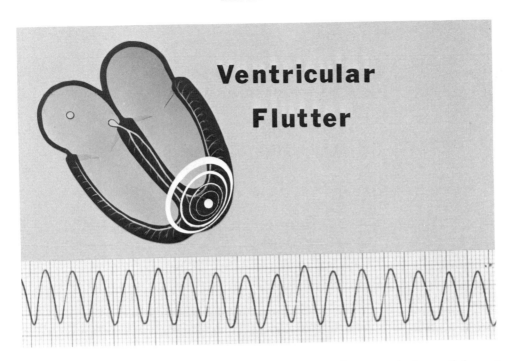

Ventricular Flutter is produced by a single ventricular ectopic focus firing at a rate of 200-300/min. Notice the smooth sine wave appearance.

Ventricular Flutter is caused by a ventricular focus discharging electrical stimuli at a rate of _____ per minute.

200-300

This extremely fast rate is dangerous. Make certain that you can recognize the smooth _____ wave appearance of the waves.

sine

NOTE: Ventricular Flutter deteriorates into deadly arrhythmias.

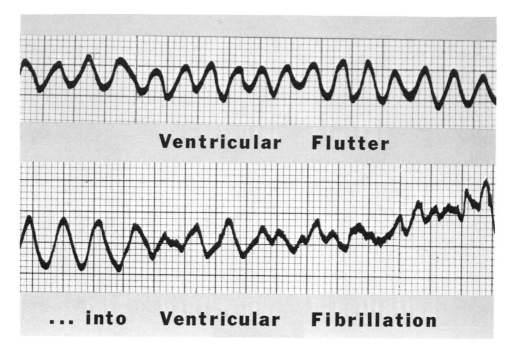

True Ventricular Flutter almost invariably becomes Ventricular Fibrillation requiring cardio-pulmonary resuscitation and defibrillation.

NOTE: During Ventricular Flutter the ventricles are contracting at an incredible rate. The above tracings show Ventricular Flutter at a rate of about 300 per minute, or 5 contractions per second. Blood is a viscous fluid and the ventricles cannot be filled at a rate of 5 times per second, so there is virtually no ventricular filling. For this reason there is no effective cardiac output. The coronary arteries are not receiving blood at this rate and the heart itself has no blood supply. Ventricular Fibrillation results as the many ventricular ectopic foci try to compensate.

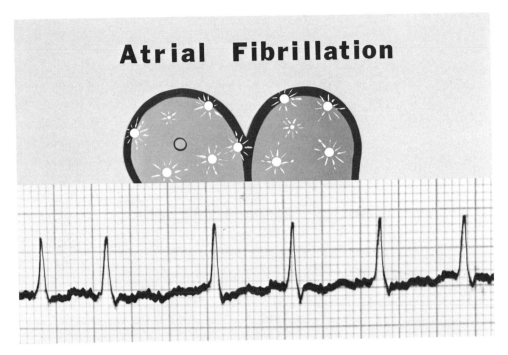

Atrial Fibrillation is caused by *many* ectopic atrial foci firing at different rates causing a chaotic, irregular atrial rhythm.

Atrial _____ occurs when many ectopic foci   fibrillation
in the atria fire continuously.

NOTE: Only a small portion of the atria is depolarized by any one ectopic impulse, and because so many ectopic foci are rapidly firing, no one discharge is carried far.

NOTE: With a normal rhythm the S A Node sends out an impulse which spreads through the atria like a circular wave caused by throwing a pebble in a still pool of water. The erratic depolarization of atrial fibrillation is analogous to numerous pebbles being thrown into different areas of the same pool at once.

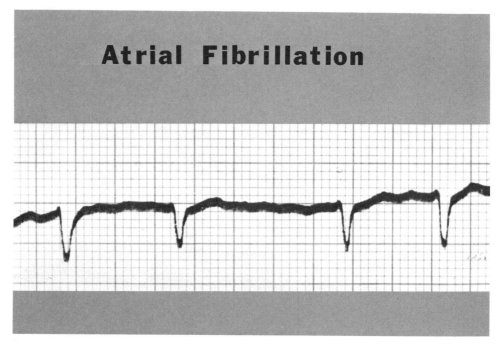

Atrial Fibrillation

Atrial fibrillation often appears only as an irregular baseline without P waves. The QRS response is *not* regular and may be rapid or slow.

Atrial fibrillation may cause such small shallow spikes that it appears as an irregular baseline without visible _____ waves.

P

The A V Node is irregularly stimulated during atrial fibrillation, so the ventricular _____ is likewise generally irregular. (Therefore expect an irregular pulse.)

response

NOTE: The ventricular rate depends on the A V Node's response to multiple small stimuli, so the ventricular rate may be rapid or relatively normal.

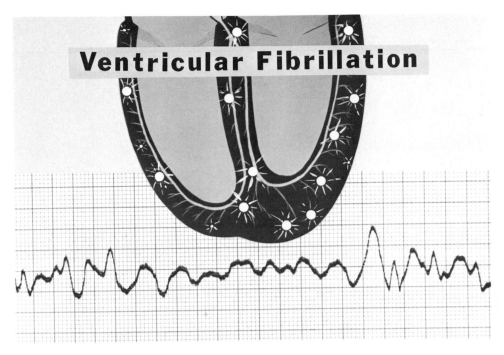

Ventricular Fibrillation

Ventricular Fibrillation is created by stimuli from many ventricular ectopic foci causing a chaotic twitching of the ventricles.

_____ fibrillation originates in numerous ventricular ectopic foci each of which fires at a certain rate.

Ventricular

Because there are so many ventricular ectopic _____ firing at once, each of which only discharges a small area of ventricle, this results in an irregular twitching of the ventricles.

foci

This chaotic twitching is often called a "bag of worms" for this is the way the ventricles really appear. There is no effective _____ pumping.

cardiac

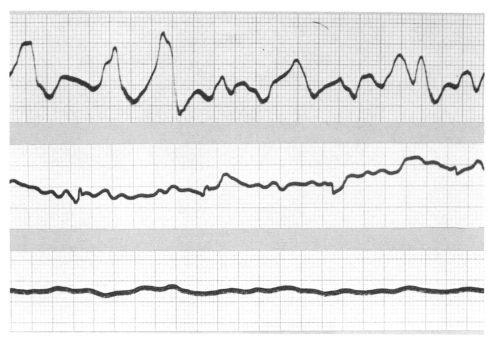

Ventricular fibrillation is easily recognized by its totally irregular appearance.

Ventricular fibrillation is easily recognized by the
totally _____ appearance on the tracing.   irregular

There is no characteristic pattern of _____   ventricular
fibrillation. As you can see, it appears different at every
moment, but it is so chaotic that it is difficult to miss.

If you *do* recognize any repetition of pattern or
regularity of deflections, you probably are not
dealing with ventricular _____.   fibrillation

NOTE: These three strips are a continuous tracing of the
same patient's dying heart. Notice how the amplitude of
the deflections becomes less as the heart dies.

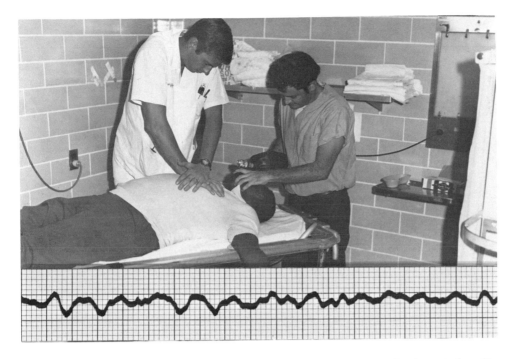

In ventricular fibrillation there is no pumping action of the heart (cardiac arrest); this is a dire emergency!

Ventricular fibrillation is a type of cardiac arrest.
There is no effective cardiac _____, because the
ventricles are only twitching irregularly, there is
no ventricular pumping - i.e. no circulation.

pumping

NOTE: The other type of cardiac arrest is standstill
(or "asystole") which occurs when there is no cardiac
activity. On EKG just flat baseline.

NOTE: Ventricular fibrillation is an emergency situation
which requires immediate care (external cardiac massage
and artificial respiration) known as Cardio-Pulmonary
Resuscitation. The technique of C.P.R. was originally
taught only to hospital and ambulance personnel, but it
is now mandatory that every living person be adept at this
technique. In this way immediate resuscitation may be
rendered to people suddenly stricken with ventricular fibrillation
in any locale or situation.

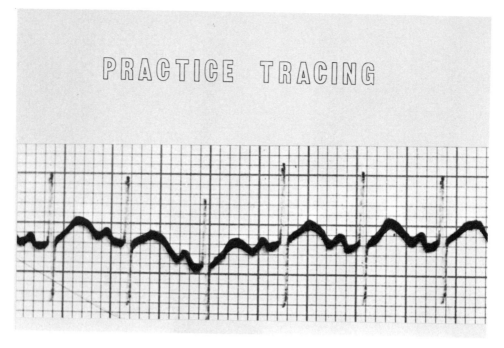

A patient became quite concerned about a sudden pounding in his chest.

This tachycardia demonstrates narrow, normal looking
QRS's, so this could not be Ventricular Tachycardia,
Ventricular Flutter, or Ventricular _____.

Fibrillation

There are P waves present, so we know that we are
not dealing with Atrial Fibrillation or (A V) Nodal
_____.

Tachycardia

There is only one P wave for each QRS, so this is not
Atrial _____.

Flutter

NOTE: This must be Atrial Tachycardia, and the history
tells us that it was paroxysmal. Could this be P.A.T.
with block? Nope!

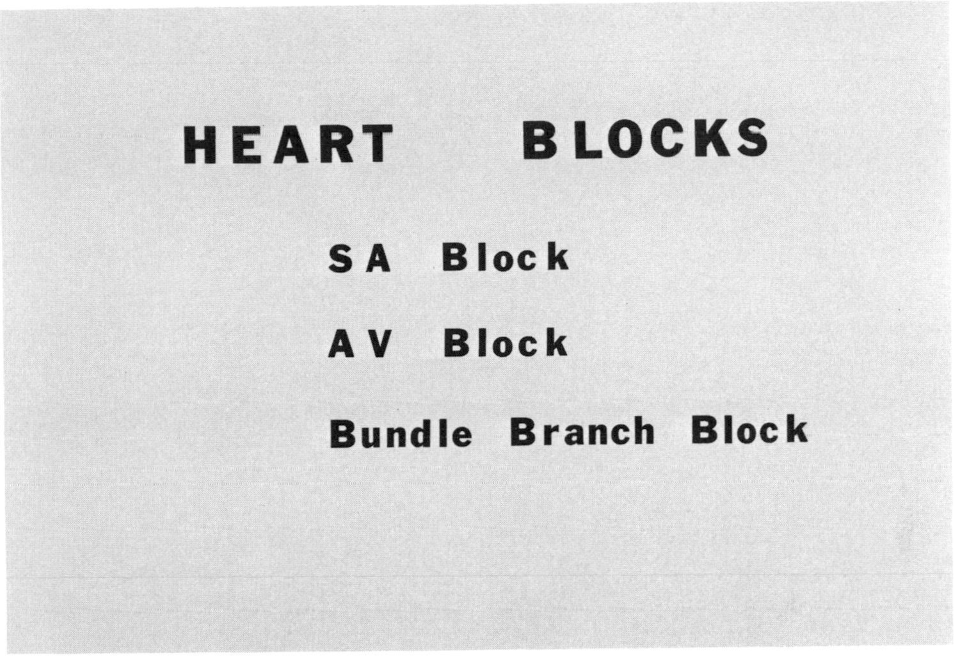

HEART   BLOCKS

S A   Block

A V   Block

Bundle   Branch   Block

Heart blocks can occur at the S A Node, A V Node, or in the Bundle Branch system.

Heart blocks may occur in any one of three areas: The S A Node, A V Node, or the _____ Branches.

Bundle

_____ blocks are electrical blocks which deter the passage of _____ stimuli.

Heart
electrical

NOTE: When checking the rhythm on a tracing you must ALWAYS check for heart blocks.

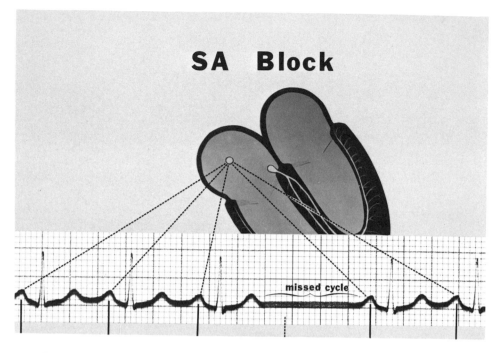

SA Block

S A (Node) *block* causes the pacemaker to temporarily stop for at least one cycle, but then the pacemaker resumes the pacing activity.

An S A Node block stops the S A Node from emitting stimuli for at least one complete _____.

cycle

After the pause the usual pace _____ with the same rhythm as prior to the block, as the same pacemaker resumes activity.

resumes

NOTE: The P waves before and after the block are identical because the same S A Node pacemaker is functioning before and after the pause (i.e. all P waves originate in the S A Node).

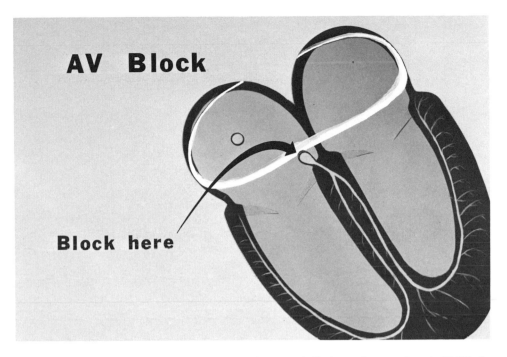

A V (Node) *block* creates a delay of the (atrial) impulse at the A V Node, making a longer-than-normal pause before stimulating the ventricles.

The A V block delays the atrial impulse before it continues to stimulate the _____.

A V Node

NOTE: You will remember the one-tenth second that we arbitrarily gave to the pause between atrial depolarization and A V Node stimulation. This pause between the P wave and QRS complex is lengthened on the EKG tracing, when an A V Block is present.

The delay is in the immediate area of the A V Node; once the A V _____ is stimulated, depolarization proceeds normally.

Node

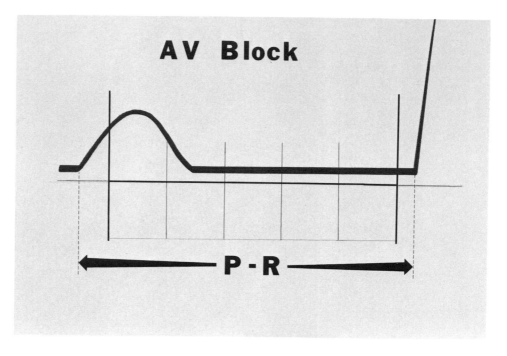

The delay of A V block prolongs the P-R interval more than one large square (.2 sec.) on EKG.

The delay caused by the A V block prolongs the
P-R _____.   interval

NOTE: Although "segments" are portions of baseline, an "interval" usually contains a wave. So the P-R interval includes the P wave and the baseline that follows it up to the point where the QRS complex begins. The P-R interval is measured from the beginning of the P wave to the beginning of the QRS complex.

The P-R interval should measure less than one large square
or less than ___ second.   .2

NOTE: You *must* measure the P-R interval on every EKG, for if the P-R interval is longer than one large square, an A V block is present.

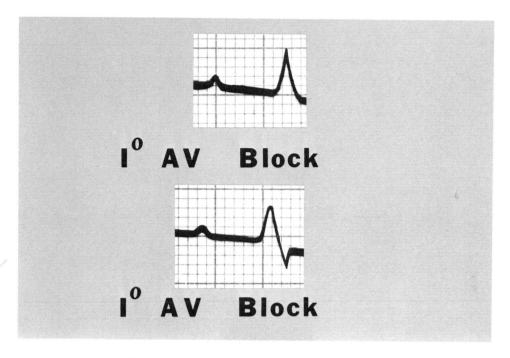

A *first degree A V Block* is characterized by a P-R interval greater than .2 sec. (one large square).

Once you recognize a prolonged P-R _____, you should determine the type of A V Block which is present.

interval

Some type of A V Block is present if the _____ interval is longer than .2 second.

P-R

A _____ degree A V Block is present when the P — QRS — T sequence is normal but the P-R interval is prolonged.

first

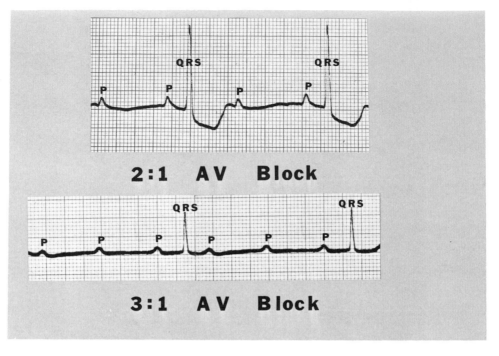

2:1 A V Block

3:1 A V Block

A *second degree A V block* is present when it takes 2 or more atrial impulses to stimulate the ventricular (QRS) response (2:1 or 3:1 block).

Occasionally it takes two or more atrial impulses to stimulate the A V Node. This is a _____ degree block.

second

This appears as two or more P waves before each _____ on the EKG tracing.

QRS

When it takes _____ atrial depolarizations (P waves) to elicit a response from the A V Node, this is a 3 to 1 (3:1) A V block.

three

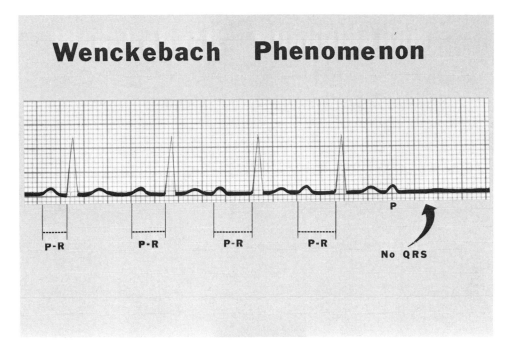

Wenckebach Phenomenon

The *Wenckebach* phenomenon occurs when the P-R interval becomes progressively longer until the A V Node is not stimulated (no QRS).

The Wenckebach phenomenon (pronounced Winky-bok)
occurs when the A V block prolongs the P-R _____
progressively with each succeeding cycle.   interval

The P-R interval becomes gradually longer from cycle to
cycle until the final P wave does not elicit a _____ response.   QRS

The P wave and QRS complex get farther apart in successive
cycles. The last P _____ stands alone.   wave

NOTE: Wenckebach phenomenon is a type of second
degree block. This is *Mobitz I.*

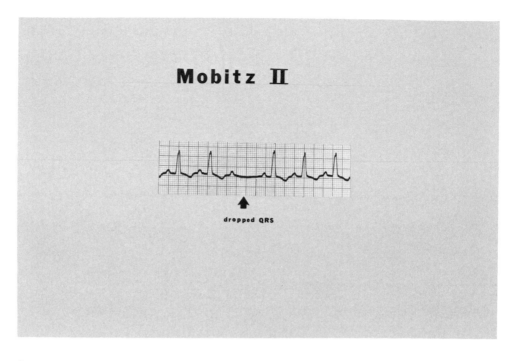

Occasionally without lengthening of the P-R interval, a QRS is dropped. This is a Mobitz II.

Mobitz II is noted when occasional ventricular depolarization is missed after a normal P wave and generally uniform P-R intervals in the _____ cycles.

preceding

NOTE: Mobitz II block often heralds serious A V Node problems with progressively more involved blocking of Nodal conduction.

An occasional dropped QRS complex may indicate a _____ block.

Mobitz II

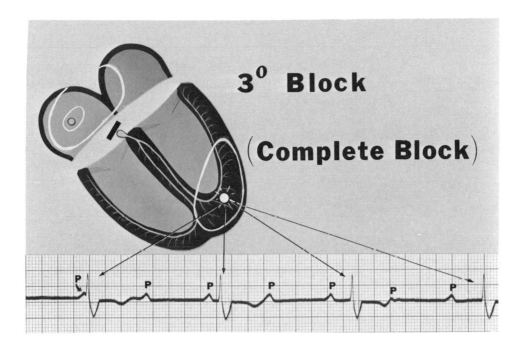

Third degree ("complete") *block* occurs when none of the atrial impulses stimulate the A V Node (no ventricular response). The ventricles must be paced independently.

In 3° (third degree) block none of the atrial depolarizations stimulate the A V _____.

Node

NOTE: In 3° block the A V block is "complete", that is, no atrial impulses get through to the A V Node. As a result, the unstimulated ventricles or A V Node call into action an ectopic pacemaker. In this case there is an atrial rate and an independent ventricular rate. If the QRS's appear normal, the rhythm is often said to be "idionodal" (A V Node pacer) and if the QRS's are wide and bizarre the rhythm is often called "idioventricular" (ventricle pacemaker). The location of the ectopic pacemaker is sometimes assumed by the ventricular rate, i.e. ventricular rate of 60- Nodal pacemaker, ventricular rate of 30-40 is a ventricular ectopic pacemaker.

One will find a certain atrial (P wave) rate and an independent, usually slower, _____ rate in third degree A V block. This is often called A V Dissociation.

ventricular
(QRS)

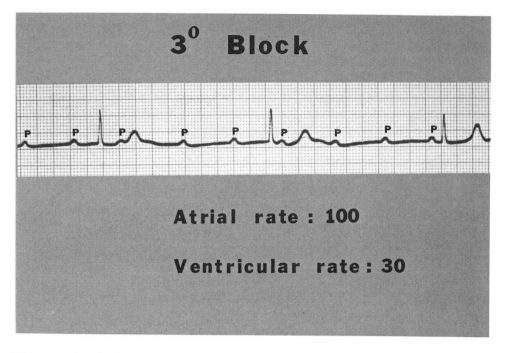

The unstimulated ventricles (in third degree block) set their own slow (30-40/min.) independent pace, or may be paced by the A V Node.

Very slow rates are calculated by taking the cycles per six second strip and multiplying by _____.

ten

In this case a _____ ectopic pacemaker is setting the ventricular rate. Notice the atrial rate.

Nodal (because the QRS's *are* normal in appearance)

NOTE: In 3° block the pulse (ventricular rate) may be so slow that the blood flow to the brain is diminished. As a result a person with 3° block may lose consciousness. This is Stokes-Adams syndrome.

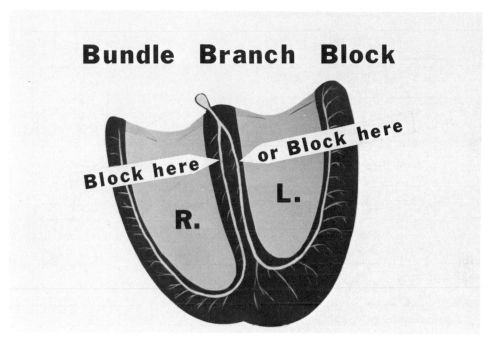

Bundle Branch Block

Bundle Branch Block is caused by a block of the impulse of the right or left Bundle Branch.

The Right Bundle Branch quickly transmits the stimulus of depolarization to the _____ ventricle. The Left Bundle Branch does the same to the left ventricle. This stimulus is transmitted to both ventricles at the same time.

right

A block to either of the Bundle Branches creates a delay of the _____ impulse to that side.

electrical

Ordinarily both ventricles are _____ simultaneously.

depolarized (or stimulated)

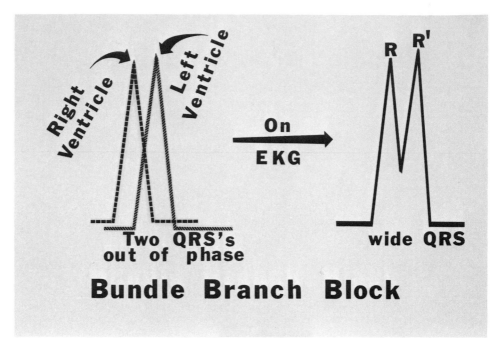

Bundle Branch Block

Therefore, in Bundle Branch Block one ventricle fires slightly later than the other, causing two "joined QRS's".

When a Bundle Branch Block is present, either the left or right _____ may fire late, depending on which side   ventricle
is blocked.

NOTE: Notice that the ventricular depolarization of both
the right and the left side are of normal duration. It is the
fact that they do not fire simultaneously that makes the
"widened QRS" appearance that we see on EKG.

Because the "widened QRS" represents the non-simultaneous
depolarization of both ventricles, one can usually see two
R _____ named in order R and R'.   waves

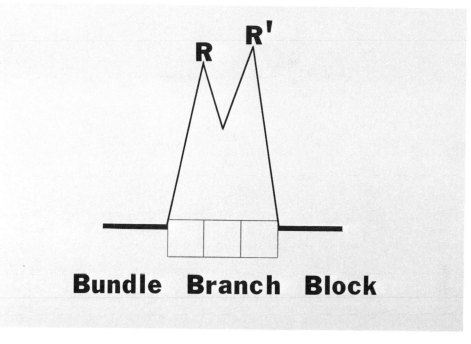

Bundle Branch Block

In Bundle Branch Block the QRS is 3 small squares wide (.12 sec.) or greater and two R waves (R and R′) are seen.

The diagnosis of Bundle Branch Block is made mainly by the widened _____.

QRS

In order to make the diagnosis of Bundle Branch Block, the QRS complex should be at least _____ small squares wide (or .12 sec.). Make certain that you check the width of the QRS routinely in every EKG that you read.

three

NOTE: The needle which records the EKG tracing moves rapidly enough to accurately record most of the heart's electrical activity. However, with great deflections the needle lags a bit mechanically. The QRS deflection in the chest leads may be so great that the needle (inaccurately) records a QRS of a longer duration than it is in reality. For this reason it is often wise to routinely check the limb leads for QRS width.

NOTE: If a patient with a Bundle Branch Block develops a supraventricular tachycardia, the rapid succession of widened QRS's may imitate Ventricular Tachycardia. Be careful!

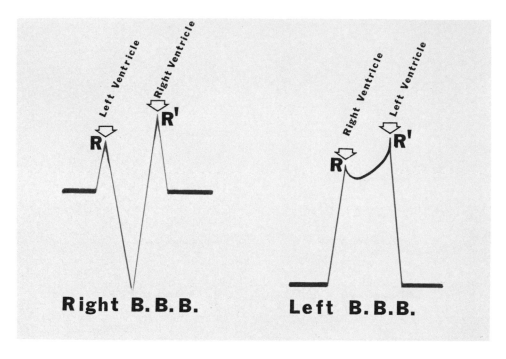

Right B.B.B.   Left B.B.B.

In Left Bundle Branch Block the left ventricle fires late; in Right Bundle Branch Block the right ventricle fires late.

In Bundle Branch Block one first notices the widened
_____. Then you should be able to find the R — R'   QRS
configuration in some leads.

In Right Bundle Branch Block the _____ ventricle fires   left
first, so the R' represents delayed activity from the
right ventricle.

In Left Bundle Branch Block the left ventricular impulse
is delayed, so the right _____ depolarizes first and   ventricle
is followed by the depolarization of the left ventricle.

NOTE: Bundle Branch Block infers a block of one branch.
Depolarization progressing down the unblocked branch creeps
around the blocked area (of the blocked branch) and produces
a (delayed) stimulus to that branch below the block.

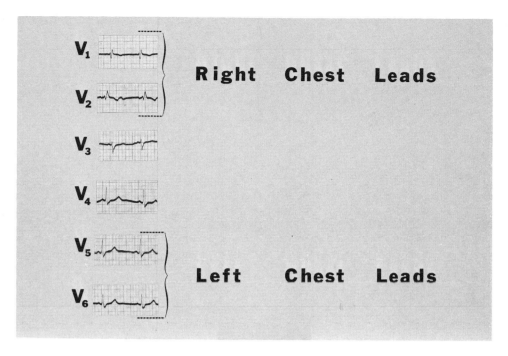

Right Chest Leads

Left Chest Leads

If there is a Bundle Branch Block, look at leads V_1 and V_2 (right chest leads) and leads V_5 and V_6 (left chest leads) for the R — R'.

When the QRS complex is wide enough to make the diagnosis of Bundle Branch Block one immediately checks the right and left chest _____ for the R — R'.

leads

NOTE: There is a very short period of time immediately after ventricular depolarization during which no stimulus can depolarize the ventricles, that is, they are refractory to any stimulus. Occasionally this refractory period varies between the two ventricles, so that during rapid rates or after early (premature) atrial beats the A V Nodal stimulus will be carried to one ventricle, and there may be a slight delay before the other ventricle responds. This unusual type of conduction called "aberrant conduction" may imitate a Bundle Branch Block.

The _____ chest leads are V_1 and V_2.

right

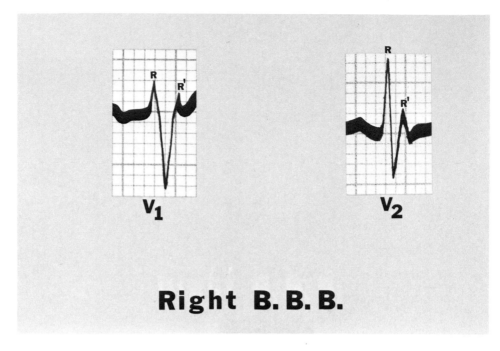

Right B.B.B.

If there is an R — R′ in V₁ or V₂ this is Right Bundle Branch Block.

With a wide _____(and a diagnosis of B.B.B.) one
checks the right and left chest leads for R — R′.

QRS

Then if there is an R — R′ in V₁ or V₂ this is probably
a _____ Bundle Branch Block.

Right

In Right Bundle Branch Block the _____ ventricle is
depolarizing slightly later than the left ventricle.

right

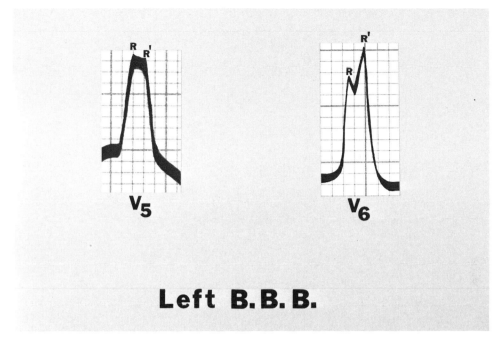

Left B.B.B.

With a Bundle Branch Block an R — R′ in the left chest leads means that Left Bundle Branch Block is present.

The left chest leads are V₅ and V₆ and the sensor electrode is over the left _____ in both leads.

ventricle

Occasionally the R — R′ will only be seen as a notch in the wide _____ in V₅ or V₆.

QRS

In Left Bundle Branch Block the _____ ventricle fires before the left ventricle, so the first portion of the wide QRS represents right ventricular depolarization.

right

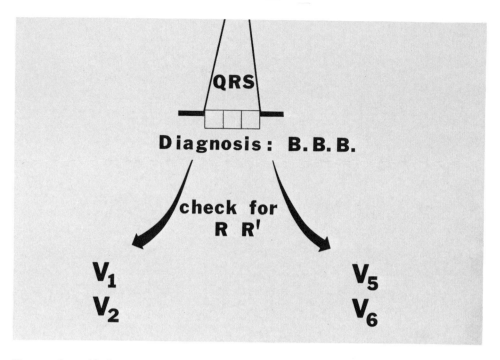

Remember, if there is a wide QRS (3 small squares), identify the type of block by checking the left and right chest leads.

To have a Bundle Branch Block the QRS must be at least _____ seconds in duration.

.12

NOTE: In some individuals a Bundle Branch Block will not become evident until a certain rapid rate has been reached. When a Bundle Branch Block only occurs at a certain rate this is called "critical rate".

The R — R' pattern may occur in only one chest _____. It is often difficult to see the R' but it can usually be found in V_1, V_2, V_5, or V_6.

lead

NOTE: Occasionally one can see an R — R' in a QRS of normal duration. This is called "Incomplete" B.B.B.

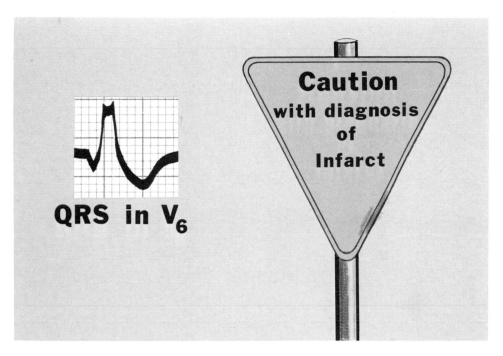

QRS in V$_6$

Caution
with diagnosis
of
Infarct

IMPORTANT: With *Left Bundle Branch Block* infarct cannot be accurately diagnosed on EKG.

NOTE: In Left Bundle Branch Block the left ventricle fires late so the first portion of the QRS complex represents right ventricular activity. Therefore we cannot identify Q waves originating from the left ventricle (which signify infarction).

In _____ Bundle Branch Block the EKG should be studied for signs for infarction as usual.

Right

NOTE: With Left Bundle Branch Block other studies are needed to verify the presence of a suspected acute infarction.

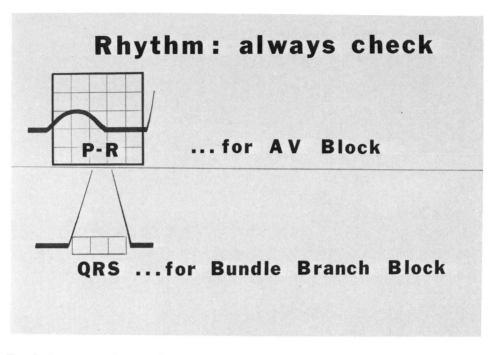

Rhythm: always check

P-R ...for AV Block

QRS ...for Bundle Branch Block

Don't forget to always check the length of the P-R interval and QRS complex when checking Rhythm.

You must always check the P-R interval on all EKG's because if it is prolonged this means that there is some kind of _____ Block present.

A V

The QRS width must also be checked on all EKG's for if it is prolonged there is a _____ _____ Block.

Bundle Branch

NOTE: Measure the P-R interval and the QRS width when checking the rhythm on any EKG. This should be a part of your normal routine. The sudden appearance of an A V Block or Bundle Branch Block often indicates impending myocardial infarction.

Bundle Branch Block

Vector : ?

Ventricular Hypertrophy?

The Mean QRS Vector and ventricular hypertrophy cannot be accurately calculated in the presence of Bundle Branch Block.

NOTE: Because the Mean QRS Vector represents the general direction of the simultaneous depolarization of the ventricles, it is very difficult to represent such a vector in B.B.B. because the ventricles are firing out of phase and there are really two (right and left) ventricular vectors.

QRS

The criteria for ventricular hypertrophy are based on a normal QRS. Bundle Branch Block produces large QRS deflections because each ventricle does not have the (usual) simultaneous electrical opposition by depolarization from the other ventricle. Therefore the EKG diagnosis of _____ hypertrophy should be very guarded.

ventricular

NOTE: In the presence of B.B.B. *atrial* hypertrophy may be diagnosed as per usual.

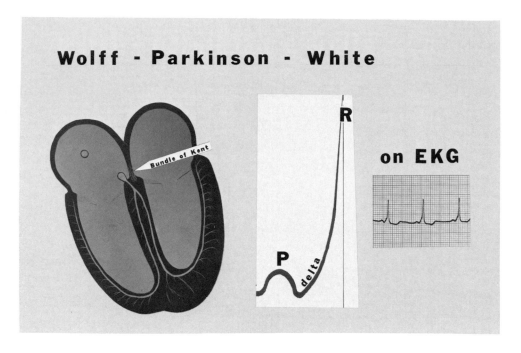

Wolff - Parkinson - White

Bundle of Kent

P delta R

on EKG

In some individuals an accessory pathway "short circuits" the (usual) delay of ventricular stimulation causing premature ventricular depolarization represented as a delta wave.

The accessory Bundle of _____ is said to provide ventricular "pre-excitation" in Wolff-Parkinson-White Syndrome.

Kent

The delta wave causes an apparent "shortened" P-R interval and "lengthened" QRS. The delta wave actually represents a _____ stimulation of a portion of the septum.

premature

NOTE: W.P.W. syndrome is very important because persons with such an accessory conduction path can have paroxysmal tachycardia of two mechanisms:

re-entry — ventricular depolarization may immediately re-stimulate the atria (and A V Node) via this accessory conduction pathway in a retrograde fashion (circus re-entry).

rapid conduction — supraventricular tachycardias (e.g. atrial flutter or atrial fibrillation) may be rapidly conducted to the ventricles 1:1 through this accessory pathway.

148

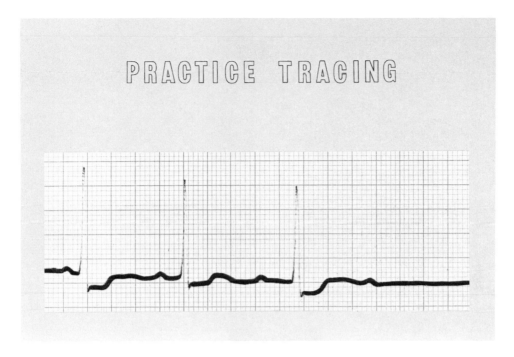

PRACTICE TRACING

An examining physician noted that this patient had an irregular pulse. He was surprised to feel three pulse beats and then a pause. This pattern repeated over and over.

A casual look at the last cycle reveals a P-R interval which is longer than .2 sec., so we suspect some kind of _____ Block.

A V

By close examination we note that the P-R interval is normal at first but becomes progressively longer with each succeeding cycle. We now suspect _____ phenomenon.

Wenckebach

After the last cycle we note a lone _____ wave with no QRS response.

P

NOTE: Review Rhythm by turning to the small notebook sheets at the end of this book (pages 270-271).

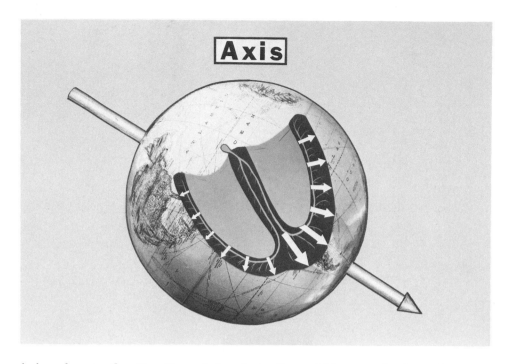

Axis refers to the direction of depolarization which spreads throughout the heart to stimulate the muscle fibers to contract.

NOTE: The axis around which the earth rotates has nothing to do with electrocardiography, but we can use the large arrow ("axis") in this picture.

Electrical _____ of the cardiac muscle fibers proceeds in a certain direction.

stimulation (depolarization)

_____ refers to the direction of this electrical stimulus.

Axis

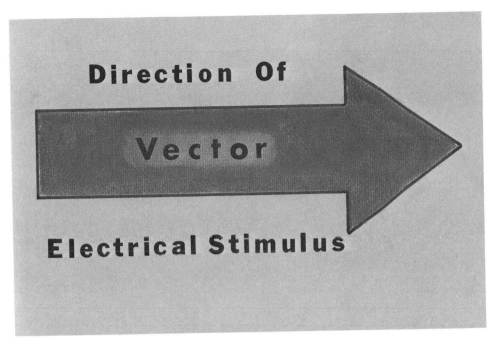

To demonstrate the direction of electrical activity, we use a "vector".

We can demonstrate the general direction of this electrical
path by a _____.

vector

This vector shows the _____ in which most of the
electrical stimulus is traveling.

direction

For interpreting EKG's, a vector shows the direction
of electrical _____.

stimulation
(or depolarization)

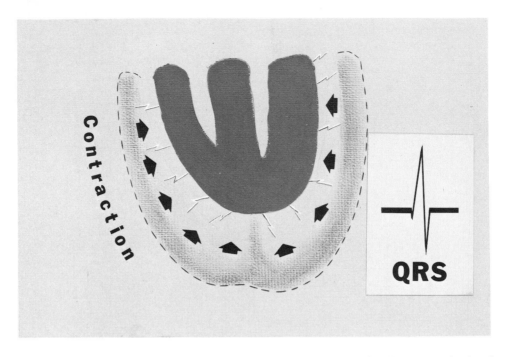

The QRS complex represents the electrical stimulation (and contraction) of the ventricles.

The _____ complex represents the simultaneous stimulation of both ventricles.   QRS

Ventricular stimulation and _____ can be said to be nearly coincident (but we know contraction lasts longer).   contraction

So the QRS complex represents _____ stimulation of the ventricles and their subsequent contraction.   electrical

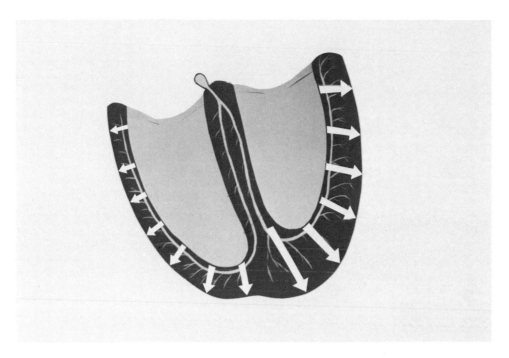

We can use small vectors to demonstrate ventricular depolarization which begins in the endocardium (inner lining) and proceeds through the ventricular wall.

NOTE: The Bundle Branch (nervous) conduction system of the ventricles transmits the electrical impulse from the A V Node to the ventricles with great speed. In this way ventricular depolarization begins within the endocardial (lining) surface and proceeds through the thickness of the ventricular wall in all areas at the same time (note small vectors as shown).

The electrical impulse of depolarization is transmitted to all areas of the endocardium (lining of both ventricles) with such great speed that _____ depolarization generally begins at the level of the endocardium in all areas at the same time.

ventricular

Depolarization of the ventricles, therefore, essentially proceeds from the _____ to the outside surface through the thickness of the ventricular wall in all areas at once.

endocardium

NOTE: Notice that the left ventricular wall has larger vectors. Also the septum depolarizes from left to right (not shown).

153

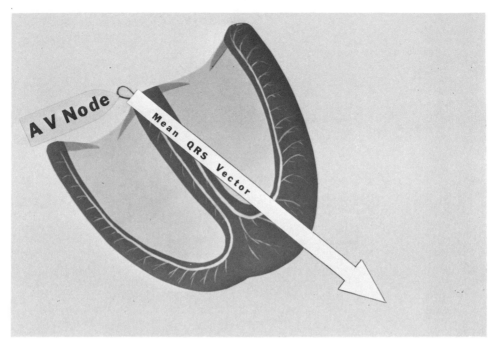

If we add up all the small vectors of ventricular depolarization (considering both direction and magnitude), we have one large "Mean QRS Vector" which represents the general direction of ventricular depolarization.

The origin of the Mean QRS Vector is always the _____.   A V Node

NOTE: The heart is the center of man, and the A V Node is the center of the heart. So the A V Node may be the center of the universe.

Because the vectors representing the depolarization of the left ventricle are larger, the Mean QRS Vector points slightly toward the left _____.   ventricle

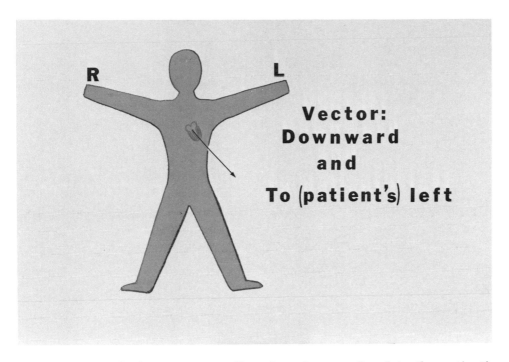

Thus the Mean QRS Vector normally points downward and to the patient's left side.

The ventricles are in the left side of the chest and angle downward and toward the _____.   left

The _____ _____ Vector points downward and toward   Mean QRS
the patient's left side.

NOTE: From now on "Vector" will imply the Mean QRS Vector. Always visualize the Vector over the patient's chest and remember that it always begins in the A V Node.

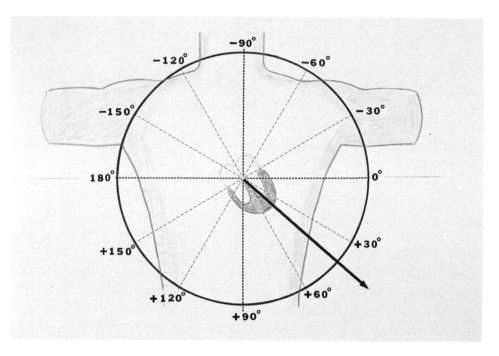

The exact position of the Mean QRS Vector is noted in degrees, in a circle drawn over the patient's chest.

We can locate the position of the Mean QRS Vector somewhere in a _____ around the heart.

circle

The center of the circle is the _____.

A V Node

The Mean QRS Vector normally points downward and to the left, or between 0 and ____ degrees.

+90
(don't forget
the +)

NOTE: The "axis" of the heart is simply the Mean QRS Vector when located by degrees in the frontal plane. For example, the axis of the heart in the above illustration is about +40 degrees.

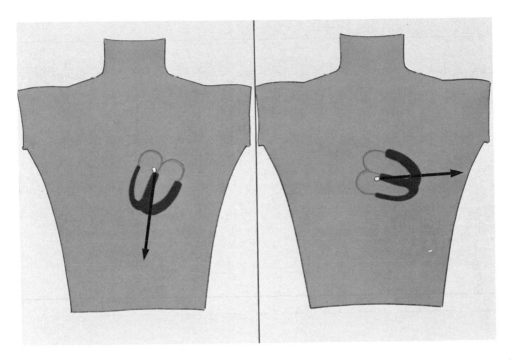

If the heart is displaced, the Vector is also displaced in the same direction. The A V Node is always the tail of the Vector.

If the heart is displaced toward the _____, the Mean QRS Vector points to the right.

right

In very fat people the diaphragm is pushed up (and so is the heart), so the Mean QRS Vector may point directly to the _____ (horizontal).

left

The tail of this Vector is always the _____.

A V Node

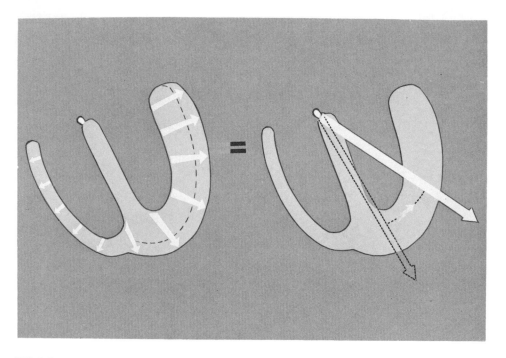

With hypertrophy (enlargement) of one ventricle, the greater electrical activity on one side displaces the vector to that side.

A hypertrophied ventricle has greater _____

electrical activity.

.... so the Mean QRS Vector is displaced toward the
_____ side.

hypertrophied

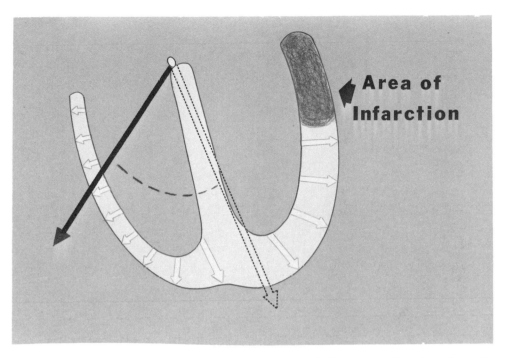

Area of Infarction

In myocardial infarction there is a dead area of the heart that has lost its blood supply and does not conduct an electrical stimulus.

NOTE: Myocardial infarction occurs when a branch of one of the coronary arteries (the only source of blood supply that the heart has) becomes occluded. The area supplied by this blocked coronary artery has no blood supply and becomes electrically dead.

In myocardial infarction (i.e. a coronary occlusion) there is an area in the heart which has no _____ supply. This infarcted area is electrically silent and therefore has no vectors.

blood

Since there is no electrical _____ in the direction of this infarcted area the Mean QRS Vector tends to point away from it, as there are no vectors there (i.e. the vectors in the opposite direction are unopposed).

activity

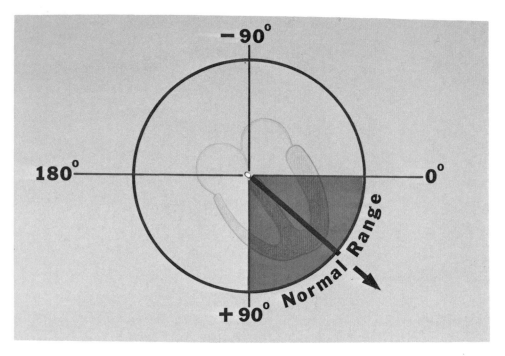

You should now see why the Mean QRS Vector gives valuable information about cardiac function.

The Mean QRS Vector should point downward to the
_____ left or in the 0 to +90 degree range.   patient's

The Mean QRS Vector gives us valuable information
about the _____ of the heart.   position

. . . . and gives insight into ventricular _____   hypertrophy
and myocardial _____.   infarction

NOTE: The Mean QRS Vector tends to point toward
ventricular hypertrophy and away from infarction.

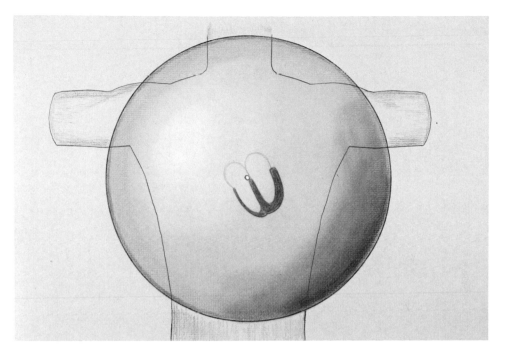

To calculate the direction of a Vector, visualize a sphere surrounding the heart with the A V Node at the center of the sphere.

Visualize a large _____ surrounding the heart.   sphere

The _____ is the center of the sphere.   A V Node

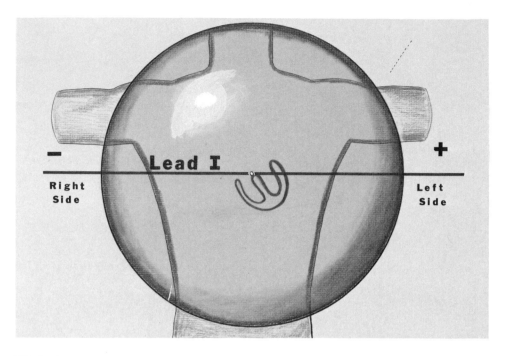

With the sphere in mind, consider lead I (left arm with the positive electrode, right arm with the negative).

Lead I uses the right and left _____ for monitoring.   arms

Introducing lead I into the sphere the left side (left arm)
is _____.   positive

In lead I the right arm is _____.   negative

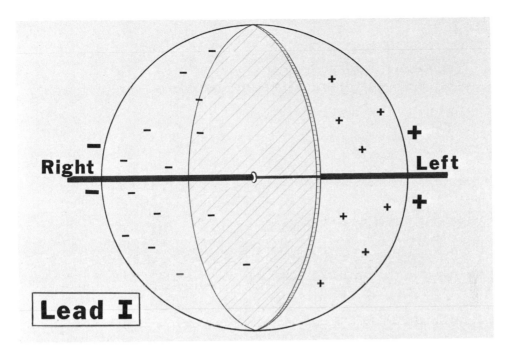

Lead I

With lead I, the patient's left hand side of the sphere is positive and the right half negative.

We can now consider the sphere in two _____.   halves

The right half of the sphere is _____.   negative

Remember we are only considering lead _____ at this time.   I

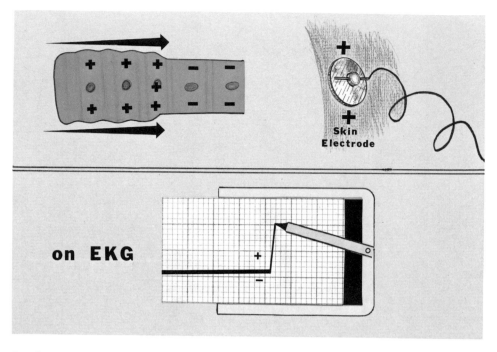

As the positive wave of depolarization within the heart cells moves toward a positive (skin) electrode, there is a positive (upward) deflection recorded on EKG.

An advancing wave of depolarization may be considered a moving wave of _____ charges.

positive

When this wave of positive charges is moving toward a positive _____ electrode, there is a simultaneous upward deflection recorded on EKG.

skin

If you see an upward wave (of depolarization) on EKG, it means at that instant there was a depolarization stimulus moving _____ a positive skin electrode.

toward

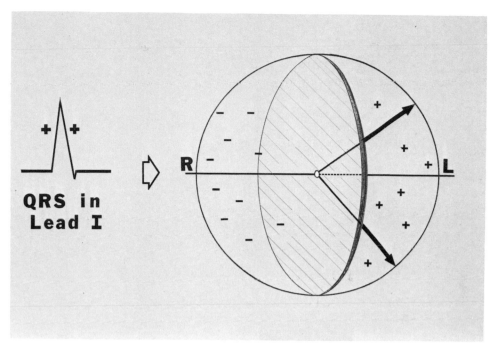

If the QRS complex is POSITIVE (mainly upward) in lead I, the Mean
QRS Vector is pointing somewhere into the left half of the sphere.

Go back to an EKG tracing and check the _____ complex   QRS
in lead I.

NOTE: We check the QRS complex because it represents
ventricular stimulation on the EKG tracing.

If the QRS in lead I is mainly upward, it is
_____ (positive or negative).   positive

.... and if the QRS is positive in lead I, then the Mean QRS
Vector points positively or into the _____ half of the   left
sphere.

NOTE: This point becomes more clear if you go back and
review the preceding page in its entirety.

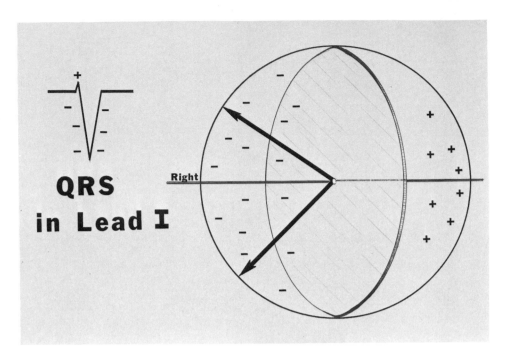

Still considering lead I on the tracing, if the QRS is mainly *negative* (downward), the Vector points to the patient's right side.

In lead I if the QRS complex is mainly below the baseline
it is _____ (positive or negative).   negative

Now checking the lead I sphere surrounding the patient, a
Vector pointing to the negative half of the sphere points
to the patient's _____ side.   right

If the QRS in lead I is mainly negative, then the
Mean _____ Vector points to the patient's right side.   QRS

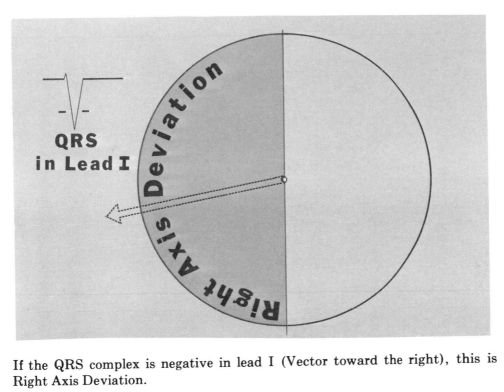

If the QRS complex is negative in lead I (Vector toward the right), this is Right Axis Deviation.

If the Mean QRS Vector points toward the right, we would expect the QRS complex in lead I to be _____.

negative

If the Mean QRS Vector points to the patient's right side (to the right of a vertical line drawn through the A V Node), this is Right _____ Deviation.

Axis

So if the QRS complex is negative in lead ____, this means that there is Right Axis Deviation.

I

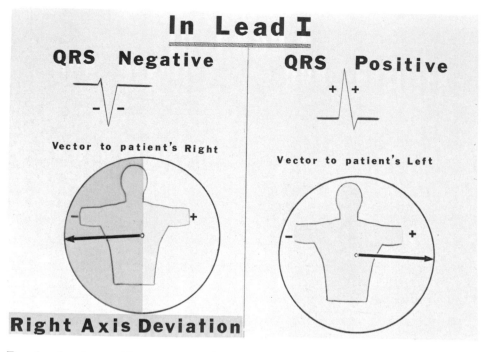

In Lead I

QRS Negative

Vector to patient's Right

QRS Positive

Vector to patient's Left

Right Axis Deviation

By simple observation we can tell whether the Mean QRS Vector points to the left or right side of the patient.

Lead _____ is the best lead to use to detect Right Axis Deviation.

I

If the QRS complex is positive in lead I (which it usually is), this means there is no R.A.D. because the Vector is pointing to the _____ side of the patient.

left

In lead I the patient's left arm carries the _____. electrode.

positive

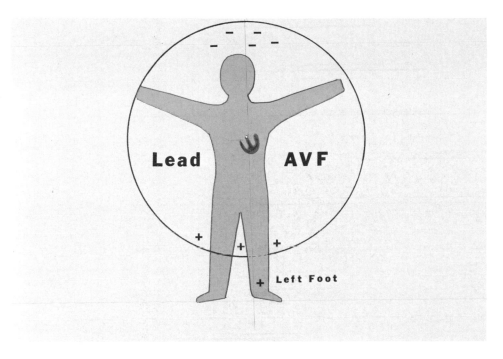

Lead AVF has a positive electrode on the left foot. Imagine a sphere around the patient for lead AVF.

Forget about the lead previously mentioned. We will only consider lead _____ at this time.

AVF

NOTE: We are now going to consider a completely different sphere — that one surrounding the body when we monitor lead AVF on the EKG machine. We will have to re-orient ourselves as to the positive and negative halves of the sphere in AVF.

When we change the EKG machine to monitor lead AVF, we make the sensor of the _____ foot positive.

left

The downward portion of the sphere is probably _____ (positive or negative).

positive

The center of the new sphere is the _____.

A V Node

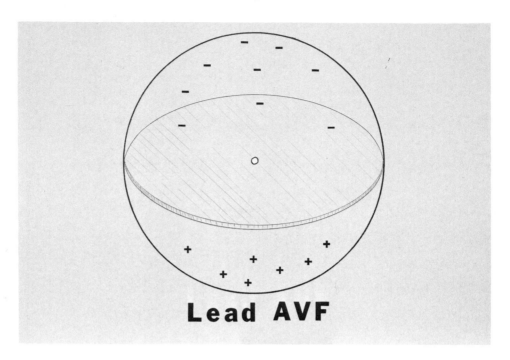

Lead AVF

For AVF the lower half of the sphere is positive, and the upper half is negative.

The upper portion of the sphere (above the A V Node) is _____ (positive or negative).

negative

The sphere in AVF is in two halves, the upper half being _____, the lower half being _____.

negative
positive

Below the A V Node the (lead AVF) sphere is _____. Reoriented now?

positive

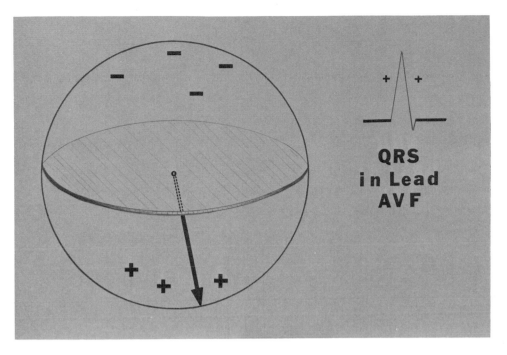

In lead AVF if the QRS is mainly positive on the tracing, then the Mean QRS Vector points downward.

In lead AVF if the Mean QRS Vector points downward, then the QRS complex on the tracing is _____.

upright or
positive

NOTE: Don't get mixed up just because the positive QRS is upright, and the Vector points downward. You must remember that the Vector is pointing into the positive half of the sphere when the QRS is positive. The lower half of the sphere just happens to be the positive half in lead AVF.

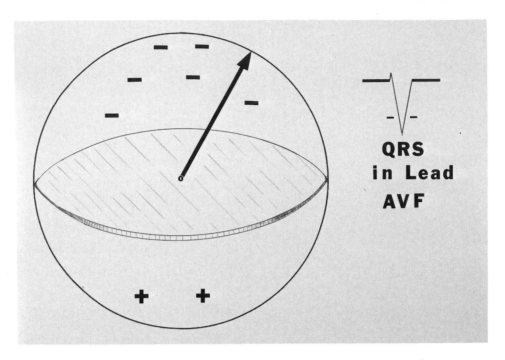

QRS
in Lead
AVF

In AVF if the QRS is negative, the Vector points upward into the negative half of the sphere.

The _____ of the sphere is the A V Node.   center

The upper half of the (lead AVF) sphere is _____ (positive or negative).   negative

A negative QRS complex in lead AVF tells us that the Mean QRS Vector points _____ into the negative half of the sphere.   upward

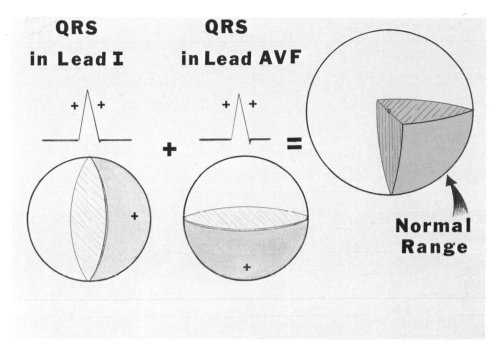

If the QRS is positive in lead 1 and also positive in AVF, the Vector points downward and to the patient's left (normal range).

A mainly positive QRS in lead I indicates that the Mean QRS Vector points to the _____ side of the patient.

left

A mainly positive QRS complex in lead AVF means that the Vector points _____.

downward

So if the QRS is positive in both leads I and AVF, the Mean QRS _____ must point downward and to the left side of the patient (and it usually does).

Vector

NOTE: The Mean QRS Vector is in the normal range when it points downward to the left, since the ventricles point downward to the patient's left. Remember that when speaking of Vector position, left or right refers to the patient's left or right side.

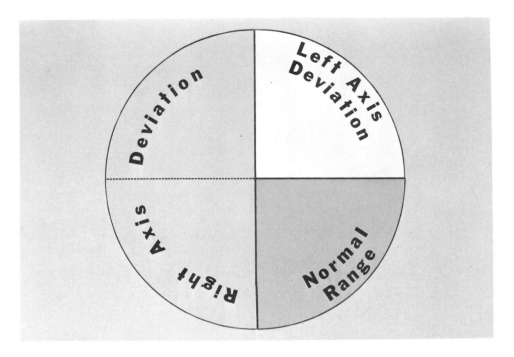

These are the four possible areas where the Mean QRS Vector may point. Visualize this over the patient's chest.

If the Vector points upward (from the A V Node) and to the patient's left, this is Left _____ Deviation.

Axis

If the Vector points to the patient's right side, this is _____ Axis Deviation.

Right

If the Vector points downward to the patient's left of the vertical it is in the _____ range.

normal

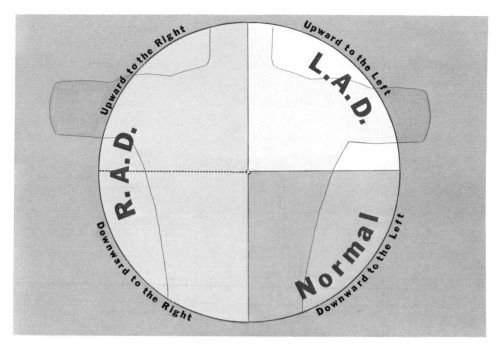

By finding into which quadrant the Vector points, we know in which direction ventricular depolarization is going.

NOTE: This is the manner in which you should visualize the four quadrants in a circle drawn around the patient's A V Node. On some EKG charts you will see a circle into which the Vector is drawn.

The upper left quadrant represents _____ Axis Deviation.

Left

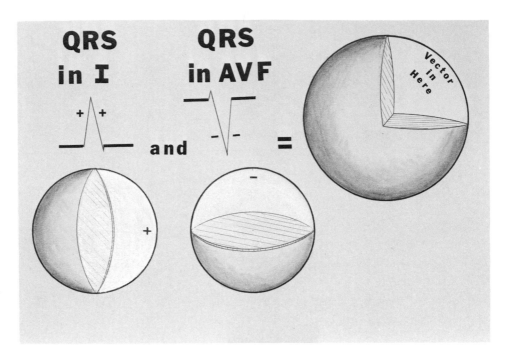

If the QRS is *positive* in lead I, and *negative* in AVF, that places the Vector in the upper left quadrant.

If the QRS in lead I is upright, the Vector points to the
_____.   left

If the Vector is pointing upwards, then the QRS in lead
AVF is mainly _____ the baseline.   below

If the Vector points upward and to the patient's left, this
is Left _____ Deviation.   Axis

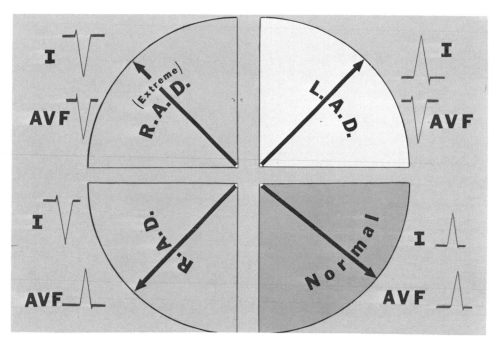

Now by looking at the QRS complex in I and AVF you can locate the Mean QRS Vector.

Any time the QRS complex is negative in lead I, there is
_____ Axis Deviation.   Right

But if the QRS is positive in lead I and negative in lead AVF, there is Left Axis _____.   Deviation

If the Mean QRS Vector points downward and to the patient's left, we would expect the QRS complexes in leads I and AVF to be mainly _____ (positive or negative).   positive

NOTE: When the Vector points upward and to the patient's right, this is often called "extreme" Right Axis Deviation.

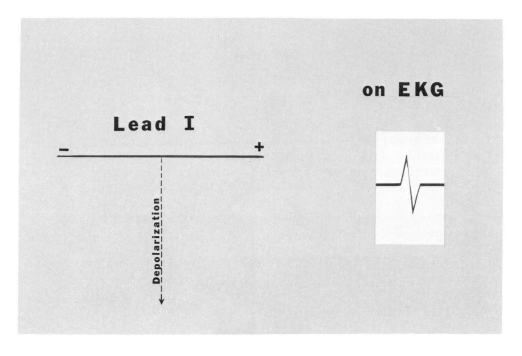

When depolarization proceeds in a direction perpendicular to the orientation of a given lead, the deflection is minimal and/or "isoelectric".

Depolarization when perpendicular to the orientation of a lead is directed negligibly toward either sensor so the recorded deflection is as much negative as positive and is called _____.   isoelectric

The word isoelectric means the "same" voltage, so positive and negative portions of the QRS complex are about _____.   equal

Although the positive and negative deflections of an isoelectric QRS are equal in magnitude, they are generally
_____.   small

NOTE: After locating the mean QRS Vector in a given quadrant (i.e. Normal, L.A.D., R.A.D., or Extreme R.A.D.), by noting the lead in which the QRS is most isoelectric, we can more precisely locate the Vector, for it will be about 90° from the orientation of the most "isoelectric" lead. (see next page).

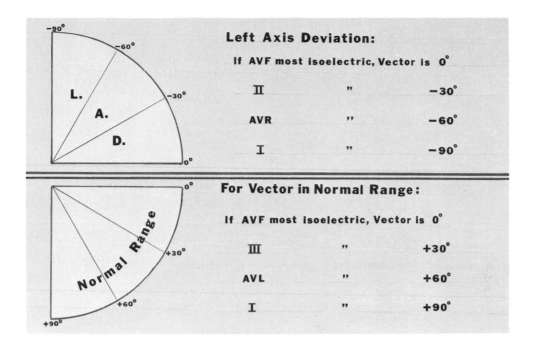

Left Axis Deviation:

If AVF most isoelectric, Vector is 0°

II	"	−30°
AVR	"	−60°
I	"	−90°

For Vector in Normal Range:

If AVF most isoelectric, Vector is 0°

III	"	+30°
AVL	"	+60°
I	"	+90°

For those who wish to locate a Vector in a more exact way (i.e. in degrees) in the frontal plane, first locate the quadrant, and then note the lead where the QRS is most isoelectric.

A patient with Left Axis Deviation would have a mean QRS Vector of between 0 and ＿＿＿＿ degrees.

-90°
(don't forget the negative)

A patient with a +60° Vector is within the ＿＿＿＿ range.

normal

A patient with a Mean QRS Vector in the normal range would have an electrical axis of +30° if the QRS in lead ＿＿＿＿ was isoelectric.

III

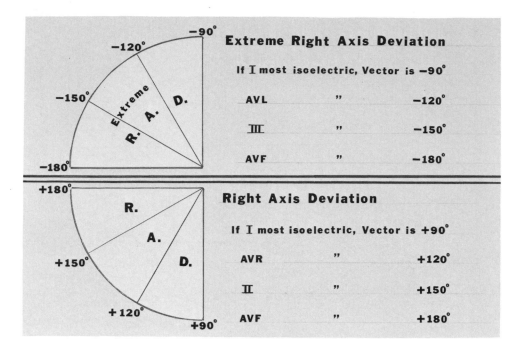

The Mean QRS Vector can be located in a similar way for Right Axis Deviation and Extreme Right Axis Deviation.

A patient with R.A.D. and a Vector of +150 degrees would probably have a tracing with an isoelectric QRS in lead _____.   II

Finding a Vector of approximately -150° would mean that the Vector is in the quadrant of _____R.A.D.   Extreme

NOTE: 180° is either + or - depending on whether the Vector is in the R.A.D. or Extreme R.A.D. quadrant respectively.

NOTE: One can calculate the Vector for a portion of a QRS complex (eg. the initial or terminal .04 sec.) in exactly the same manner as for the Mean QRS Vector.

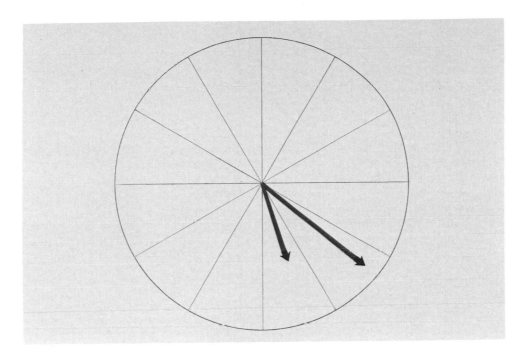

The axis is often recorded like the hands of a clock, the longer arrow is the QRS Vector, the shorter is the T wave Vector.

The T wave has a vector which can be located in the same manner as one uses for the _____ Vector.

QRS

NOTE: When the T wave and QRS Vectors are separated by 60° or more, this generally signifies pathology.

The T wave Vector is usually represented as a _____ arrow than the QRS Vector.

smaller

NOTE: Axis is often noted in the literature by A as in A +60°.

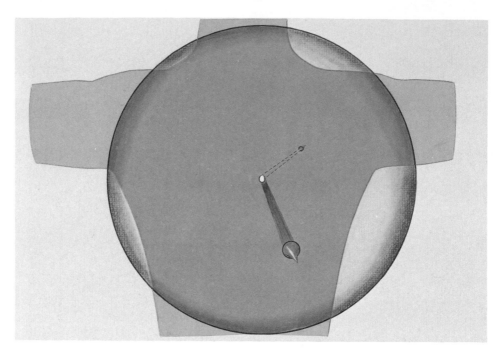

There are still 3 dimensions to the sphere, and we can locate the Mean QRS Vector as pointing forward or backward.

The Mean QRS Vector may point toward the front or
_____ of the patient.   back

This means that ventricular depolarization proceeds
forward or backward from the _____.   A V Node

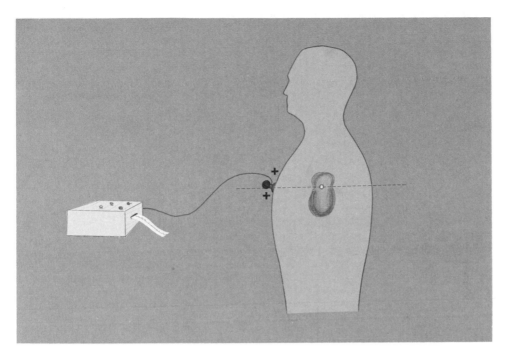

Lead V_2 is obtained by placing an electrode sensor on the chest just over the A V Node.

The electrode sensor for lead V_2 is _____ (positive or negative).

positive

NOTE: The sensor electrode for the chest leads is on a suction cup which is moved to a different position on the chest for each of the six chest leads, but in each case the suction cup sensor is positive.

The position of the sensor for lead V_2 places it directly in front of the _____ Node.

A V

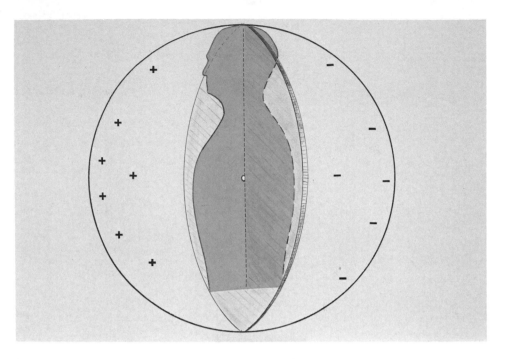

Considering a sphere for lead V_2 we can see that the front half is positive and the back half is negative.

Considering a sphere for lead V_2, we will view the patient
from the side, but the _____ of the sphere is still the   center
A V Node.

The patient's back is considered _____ (positive or   negative
negative) when considering lead V_2.

The area in front of the A V Node is in the _____ half   positive
of the sphere.

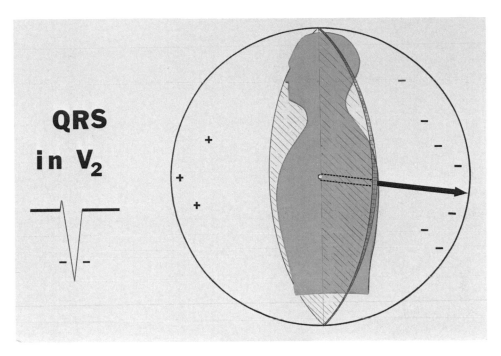

If the QRS in lead V_2 is negative, the Mean QRS Vector points backward.

The QRS complex in lead V_2 is usually _____ (or below the baseline).

negative

Therefore the Mean QRS Vector usually points _____ into the negative half of the sphere.

backward

A positive QRS in the tracing of lead V_2 means that the Mean QRS Vector is pointing _____ (and that's *not* normal).

forward

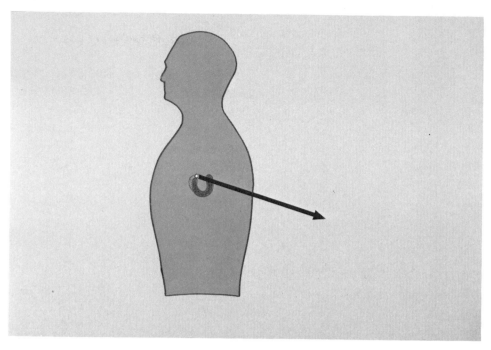

Because the thick left ventricle is posteriorly located in the chest, this draws the Vector posteriorly.

The _____ ventricle is the thicker of the two ventricles.   left

The left ventricle is more _____ in the chest than   posterior
the right ventricle.

The thicker left ventricle draws the _____ QRS Vector   Mean
toward the patient's back.

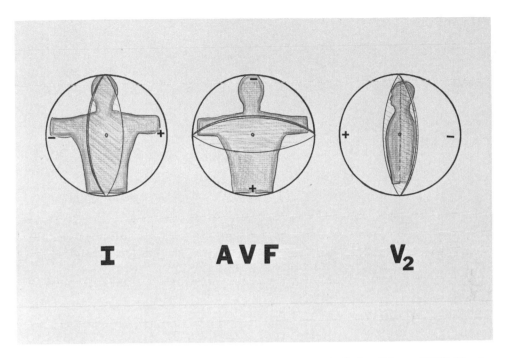

I   **AVF**   **V$_2$**

Considering only leads I, AVF, and V$_2$, you can find the Mean QRS Vector in 3-D.

The Mean QRS Vector can be located in the flat plane over the patient's chest by checking leads _____ and _____.   I and AVF

If the QRS complex in these two leads is _____, then the Mean QRS Vector is within the normal range.   positive

The Mean QRS Vector points anteriorly if the QRS complex is positive in lead _____.   V$_2$

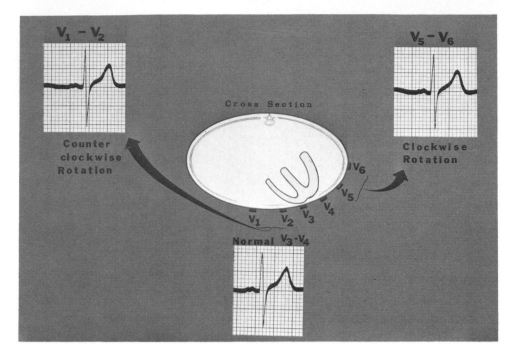

Rotation of the Vector around a central axis is sometimes referred in terms of clockwise (posterior) or counter-clockwise (anterior) rotation.

NOTE: If we could drive an iron bar in a straight line through the superior vena cava and down the inferior vena cava, the heart could rotate a little around the bar. We can determine this kind of rotation on the EKG. Similarly we can find Vector rotation around this central axis. Cardiologists know that the septal leads V_3 or V_4 have a QRS which is as much positive as negative ("transitional zone"). When the "transitional zone" QRS moves posteriorly toward leads V_5 or V_6, this is called clockwise rotation. If we see a transitional QRS (or "isoelectric QRS") in leads V_1 or V_2, this is counter-clockwise rotation.

NOTE: When we note clockwise or counter-clockwise rotation, this is rotation within the horizontal plane. Check page 38 to refresh your memory. Axis *deviation* is in the frontal plane, while *rotation* is in the horizontal plane. Review Axis by turning to the small notebook sheets at the end of this book (page 272).

Hypertrophy

Hypertrophy usually refers to an increase in size, and when relating to muscle this term refers to increase in muscle mass.

NOTE: This picture is the arm of a weight lifting enthusiast. I had contemplated using a picture of my own arm, but I soon abandoned the idea because I would then have to title this section "hypotrophy" (if there is such a word).

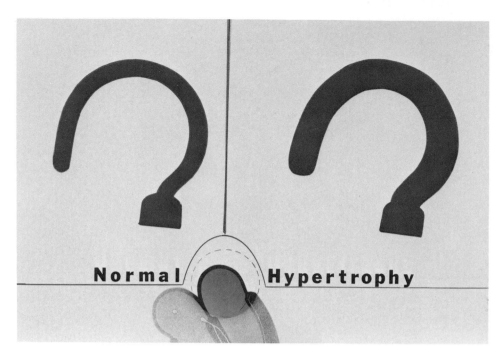

Hypertrophy of a chamber of the heart refers to an increase in the thickness of the wall of that chamber.

Hypertrophy of a chamber of the heart means that the thickness of the muscular wall of that chamber has increased beyond the _____ thickness.

normal

Hypertrophy does not usually change the volume which the _____ contains, nor does the general size necessarily dilate.

chamber

The increase in the muscular thickness of the wall of a given chamber of the heart may be diagnosed on _____.

EKG

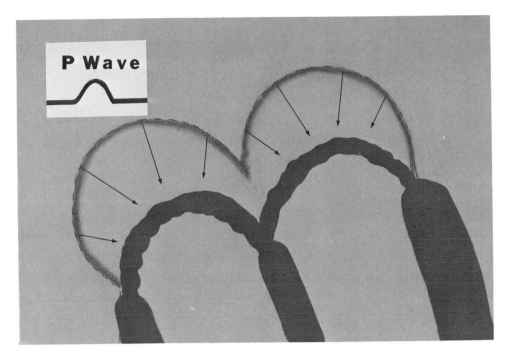

Since the P wave represents the contraction of both atria, we examine the P wave for evidence of atrial hypertrophy.

The depolarization of both atria causes their _____.   contraction

The depolarization of both atria is recorded on EKG as
a _____ wave.   P

Signs of _____ hypertrophy can be noted by examining   atrial
the P wave on the EKG tracing.

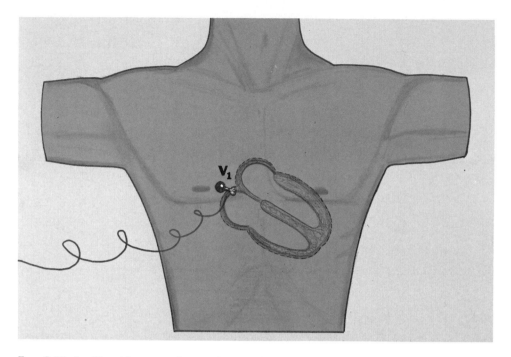

Lead V_1 is directly over the atria, so the P wave in V_1 is our best source of information about atrial enlargement.

The sensor electrode which is placed on the chest when recording lead V_1 is considered _____ (positive or negative).

positive

Lead V_1 is recorded by placing an electrode just to the right of the sternum and in the 4th interspace; this places our suction cup sensor directly over the _____.

atria

Because this electrode is closest to the atria, lead V_1 should be the most valuable lead to check for atrial _____.

hypertrophy

So one would expect the P wave in lead___ to give us the most accurate information about atrial hypertrophy — and it does!

V_1

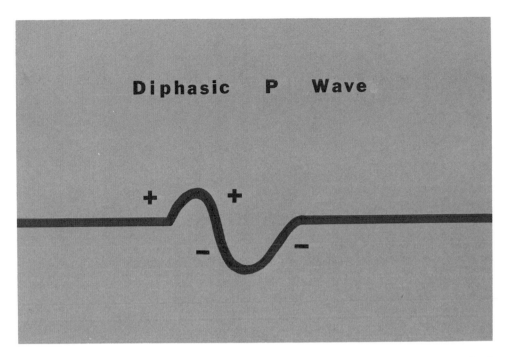

With atrial hypertrophy, the P wave is diphasic (both positive *and* negative).

A wave which has both positive and negative portions
is called a _____ wave (two phase wave).   diphasic

By diphasic we mean that the same wave has deflections
_____ and below the baseline.   above

The diphasic P wave is characteristic of atrial hypertrophy,
but we want to know which _____ is hypertrophied.   atrium

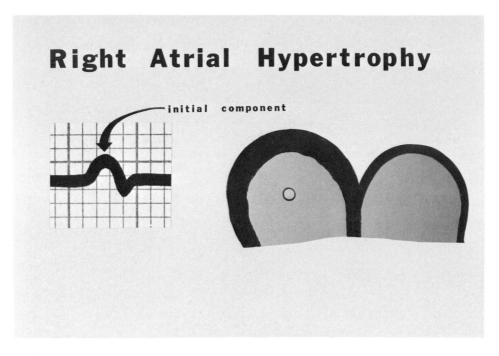

If the initial component of a diphasic P wave (in V_1) is largest, this is *Right Atrial Hypertrophy*.

If the P wave in lead V_1 is _____, then we know that one of the atria is hypertrophied.   diphasic

If the _____ portion of the diphasic P wave is the largest of the two phases, then there is Right Atrial Hypertrophy.   initial

A diphasic P wave in V_1, with a large initial component tells us that this patient's _____ atrium is thicker than his left.   right

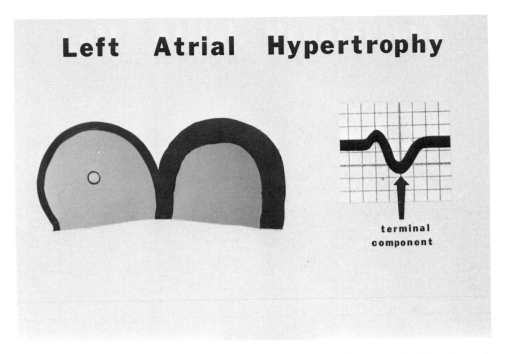

Left Atrial Hypertrophy

terminal
component

If the terminal portion of a diphasic P wave in V_1 is large and wide, there is
Left Atrial Hypertrophy.

A patient who has hypertrophy of the left atrium because
the mitral (outflow) valve is narrowed will have a diphasic
P wave in lead ____. V_1

The _____ component of this patient's P wave in V_1 terminal
is the largest component.

The terminal component of a diphasic P wave in lead V_1 is
usually _____ (positive or negative).   negative

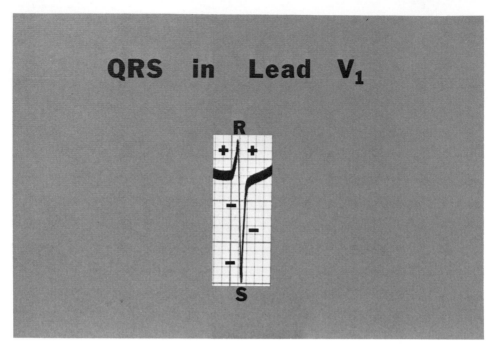

Considering the QRS complex in V_1, the S wave is normally larger than the R wave.

The QRS complex represents ventricular activation, so we would expect it to reflect some indications of the presence of _____ hypertrophy.

ventricular

In lead V_1 the QRS complex is mainly negative, and the ____ wave is therefore usually very short.

R

NOTE: The V_1 electrode is positive. Ventricular depolarization moves downward to the patient's left side and posteriorly (the thicker left ventricle is posteriorly located). Because ventricular depolarization is moving AWAY from the V_1 (positive) electrode, the QRS in V_1 is usually mainly negative. Remember that the Positive depolarization wave moving toward a Positive electrode records a Positive deflection on the EKG tracing. Similarly, depolarization moving *away* from a positive electrode records negatively.

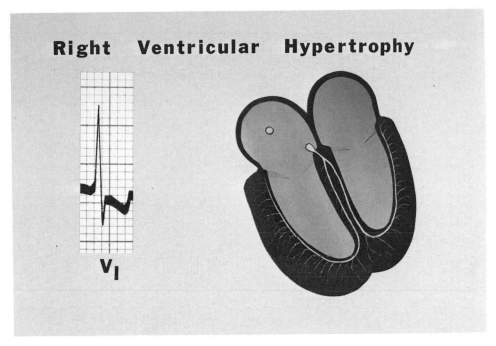

However, in *Right Ventricular Hypertrophy* there is a large R wave in V_1.

In Right Ventricular Hypertrophy there is a large _____ wave in lead V_1.

R

NOTE: With Right Ventricular Hypertrophy the wall of the right ventricle is very thick, so there is much more (positive) depolarization (and more vectors) toward the (positive) V_1 electrode. We would therefore expect the QRS in lead V_1 to be more positive (upward) than usual.

The S wave in lead V_1 is _____ than the R wave in Right Ventricular Hypertrophy.

smaller

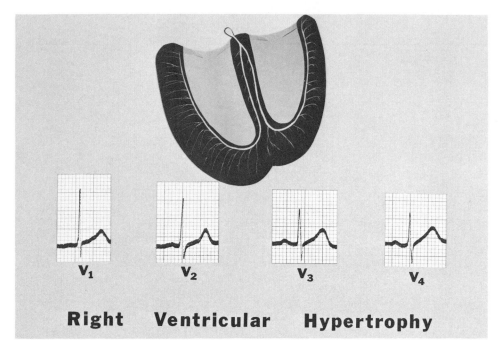

Right Ventricular Hypertrophy

In Right Ventricular Hypertrophy, the large R wave of V_1 gets progressively smaller in V_2, V_3, V_4, etc.

When Right Ventricular Hypertrophy is present, there is a large R wave in lead _____ which becomes progressively smaller in the following chest leads.

V_1

The progressive decrease in the height of the _____ wave is gradual proceeding from the right chest leads to the left chest leads.

R

NOTE: The enlarged right ventricle adds more vectors toward the right side, so there is often Right Axis Deviation (of the Mean QRS Vector) as well.

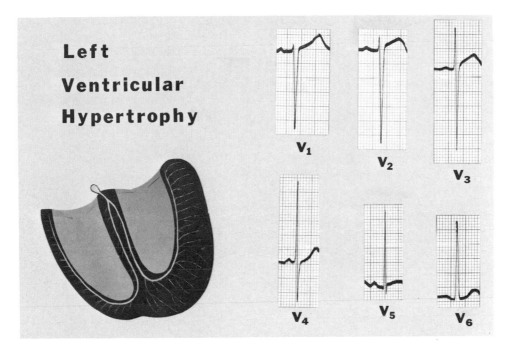

Left Ventricular Hypertrophy

V_1 V_2 V_3 V_4 V_5 V_6

In Left Ventricular Hypertrophy, the left ventricular wall is very thick causing great QRS deflections (chest leads).

The wall of the _____ ventricle is the thickest of all heart chambers.

left

Hypertrophy of the left ventricle causes QRS complexes which are exaggerated in both height and depth especially in the _____ leads.

chest

NOTE: Normally the S wave in lead V_1 is deep. But with Left Ventricular Hypertrophy even more depolarization is going downward to the patient's left — away from the positive V_1 electrode. Therefore the S wave will be even deeper in V_1. There may also be Left Axis Deviation as the Mean QRS Vector moves leftward.

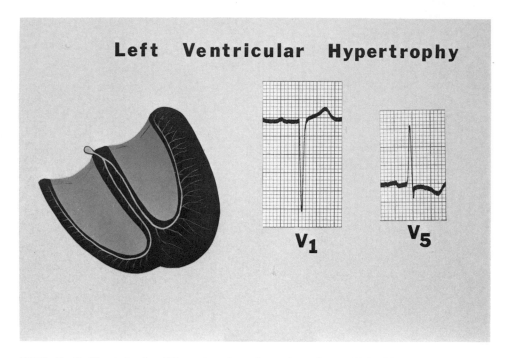

With Left Ventricular Hypertrophy there is a large S in V_1 and a large R in V_5.

With Left Ventricular Hypertrophy there is a deep _____ wave in lead V_1.

S

NOTE: Lead V_5 is over the Left Ventricle, so the increased depolarization is going toward the electrode of lead V_5 when there is L.V.H. This results in more (positive) depolarization going toward the (positive) electrode of V_5, so the QRS in lead V_5 should be mainly positive, and this results in a very tall R wave in this lead.

In Left Ventricular Hypertrophy there is a deep S wave in V_1 and a tall R wave in _____.

V_5

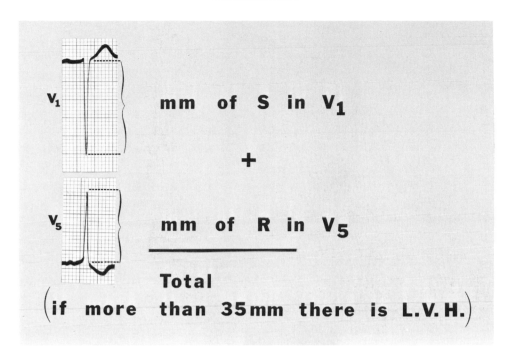

$$\text{mm of S in } V_1$$

$$+$$

$$\text{mm of R in } V_5$$

$$\overline{\text{Total}}$$

$$\left(\text{if more than 35mm there is L.V.H.}\right)$$

Depth (in mm) of S in V_1 plus the height of R in V_5 ... if greater than 35 mm there is Left Ventricular Hypertrophy.

To check an EKG for Left Ventricular Hypertrophy one must add the depth of the S wave in V_1 to the height of the _____ wave in V_5.

R

If the depth (in mm) of the S wave in V_1 added to the height of the R wave (in mm) in V_5 is greater than 35, then Left Ventricular _____ is present.

Hypertrophy

NOTE: This addition of S in V_1 plus R in V_5 should be routinely checked (mere observation will usually tell) in every EKG.

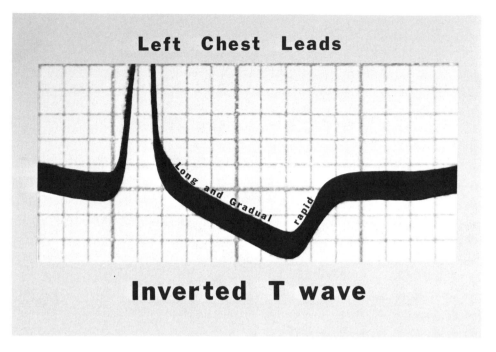

The T wave often shows "Left Ventricular Hypertrophy" characteristics. There is T wave inversion and asymmetry.

There is a characteristic _____ wave which can usually be seen when Left Ventricular Hypertrophy is present.

T

Since the left chest leads (V_5 or V_6) are over the _____ ventricle these are ideal leads to check for this T wave which indicates L.V.H.

left

This inverted T wave has a gradual downslope and a very steep return to the _____.

baseline

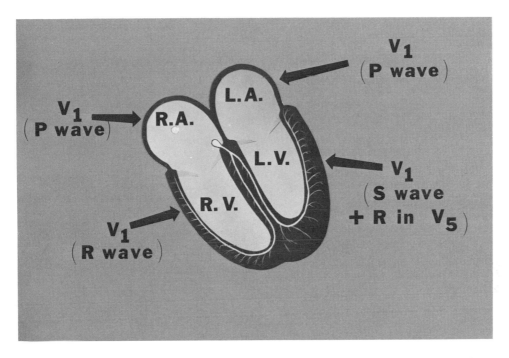

Note that most of the information concerning hypertrophy of heart chambers is gained from V_1.

When routinely reading a tracing you should check to see if there is _____ of any of the chambers.

hypertrophy

First, check the P wave in lead V_1 to see if it is _____.

diphasic

Second, check the R wave in V_1, and then check the S wave in V_1 and the _____ wave in V_5.

R

NOTE: Review Hypertrophy by turning to the small notebook sheets at the end of this book (page 273).

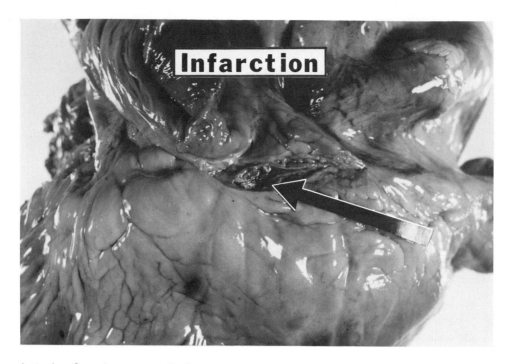

Infarction

Arteriosclerosis may occlude a coronary artery, or an arteriosclerotic plaque may be the seat of a thrombus which occludes a coronary. Coronary occlusion causes Myocardial Infarction.

NOTE: Myocardial Infarction results from an occlusion of a coronary artery. An area of the heart is then without blood supply. This type of occlusion may be relative in that a person with severely narrowed coronary arteries may function well at rest. But with excitement or exertion the rapidly pumping heart demands a greater blood (and oxygen) supply that his coronaries cannot deliver. This type of Myocardial Infarction can be just as serious or deadly as can a classical coronary occlusion.

NOTE: This section is called *Infarction* which infers a complete occlusion of a coronary artery. We can also determine whether a coronary artery is somewhat narrowed, rendering a decreased blood supply to the heart. Therefore keep in mind that we read the electrocardiogram to determine the status of coronary perfusion of the heart.

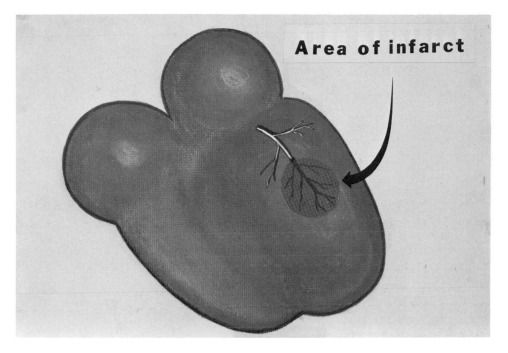

Area of infarct

Myocardial Infarction occurs when a coronary artery to the left ventricle becomes occluded, producing an area of myocardium without blood supply.

The terms heart attack, _____ occlusion, and myocardial infarction refer to the same serious phenomenon.

coronary

The heart derives its only blood supply from the _____ arteries, and when a branch of a coronary artery narrows markedly or is blocked, the area of myocardium which this branch supplies is without adequate circulation.

coronary

This "infarcted" area is usually in the left ventricle and serious arrhythmias or _____ may result.

death

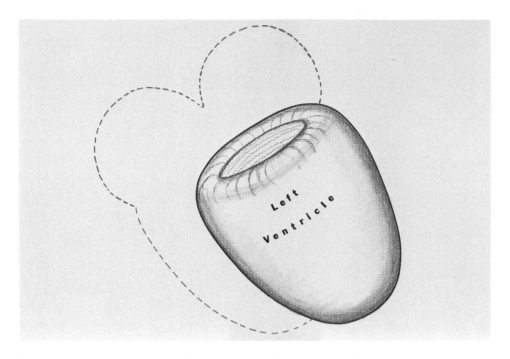

Note that only the thick *left* ventricle suffers myocardial infarction.

The left ventricle is the thickest chamber of the heart; so if
the coronary arteries are narrowed, the left ventricle,
which needs the greatest blood supply, is the first to suffer
from diminished _____ circulation.

coronary

The blood is pumped to all parts of the body by the heavy
_____ ventricle. It is pretty darn important.

left

NOTE: When we describe infarcts by location, we therefore
are speaking of an area within the left ventricle. Arteries
to the left ventricle may send branches to other areas of the
heart, so an infarction of the left ventricle can include a
small area of another chamber.

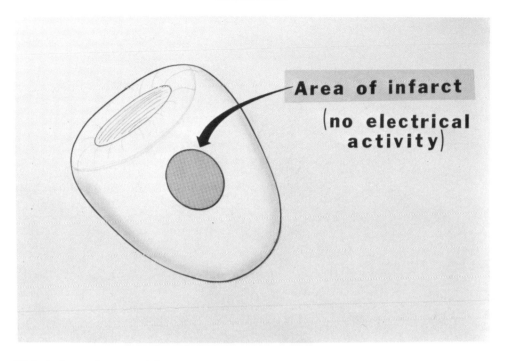

This infarcted area of left ventricle with no blood supply is electrically dead and cannot conduct electrical impulses.

Infarctions generally occur only within the wall of the left _____.

ventricle

An area of infarction conducts no _____ impulses because the cells are dead and cannot depolarize normally.

electrical

NOTE: This infarcted area produces an electrical void as the rest of the heart (with an adequate blood supply) functions as usual.

Ischemia

Injury

Infarction

The classical triad of an acute myocardial infarction is "ISCHEMIA", "IN-JURY", and "INFARCTION", but any of these three may occur alone.

The "three I" triad is the basis for recognizing and diagnosing the signs of _____ infarction.

myocardial

_____ means literally reduced blood, referring to poor blood supply.

Ischemia

NOTE: Ischemia, Injury, and Infarction need not all be present at once to establish the diagnosis of myocardial infarction, but rather provide a good set of criteria to routinely check.

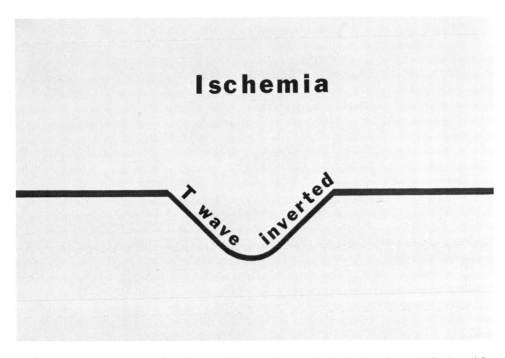

Ischemia (decreased blood supply) is characterized by inverted (upside-down) T waves.

Ischemia means reduced _____ supply (from the coronary arteries) or less than is normally present.

blood

T wave _____ is the characteristic sign of Ischemia and may vary from a slightly flat or depressed wave to deep inversion.

inversion

Inverted _____ waves may indicate ischemia in the absence of myocardial infarction. There can be a reduced blood supply to the heart without creating an infarction.

T

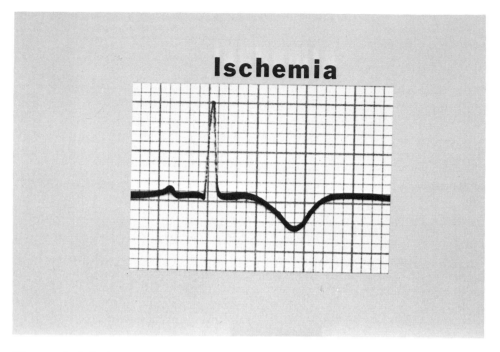

The typical Ischemia T wave is symmetrically inverted.

NOTE: With every EKG you should routinely check for T wave inversion. Since the chest leads are nearest the ventricles, T wave changes will be most pronounced in these leads. Always run down V_1-V_6 and check for T wave inversion to see if there is diminished coronary blood flow.

The T wave of Ischemia is inverted and is_____.

symmetrical.

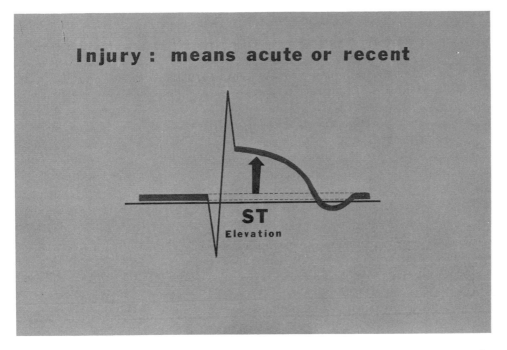

Injury : means acute or recent

ST
Elevation

"INJURY" indicates the acuteness of an infarct. ST segment elevation denotes "injury".

The ST segment is that section of baseline between the
QRS complex and the _____ wave.

T

Elevation of the _____ segment signifies "injury". The ST
segment may be only slightly elevated, or as much as ten
or more millimeters above the baseline.

ST

The _____ of the ST segment gives us evidence
that an infarct is acute.

elevation

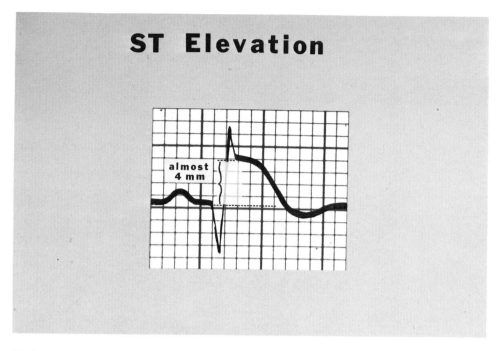

If there is ST elevation this means that the infarction is fresh (acute).

NOTE: If you have made the diagnosis of infarction,
it is important to know whether the infarction just occurred
and needs immediate treatment, or if the infarction is old —
maybe years old.

The ST _____ rises above the baseline with an acute   segment
infarction and later returns to the level of the baseline.

NOTE: Pericarditis may elevate the ST segment, however
the T wave is usually elevated off the baseline also.

NOTE: A ventricular aneurysm (the outward ballooning of
the wall of a ventricle) may also cause ST elevation, but the
ST segment in this case does not return to the baseline
with time.

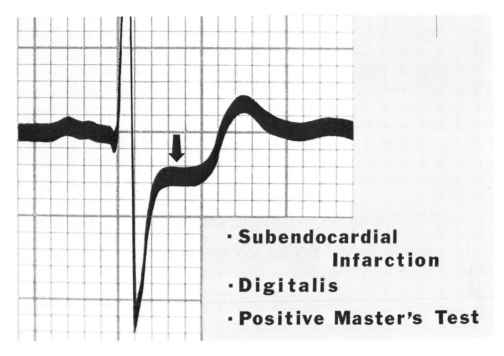

· Subendocardial
Infarction
· Digitalis
· Positive Master's Test

The ST segment may be depressed in certain conditions.

Digitalis may cause _____ of the ST segment.   depression

When a patient with suspected coronary Ischemia is
exercised, depression of the _____ segment may occur   ST
confirming the diagnosis (Master Test).

A _____ infarction — an infarct which does   subendocardial
not involve the full thickness of the left ventricle — will
depress the ST segment.

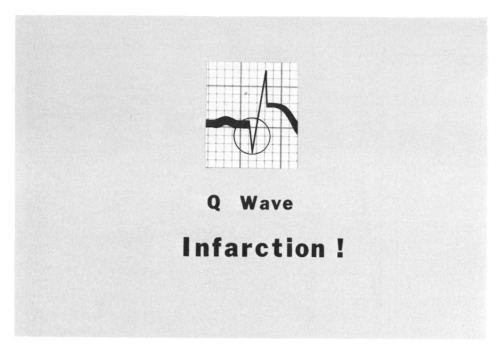

Q Wave

Infarction !

The Q wave makes the diagnosis of infarction.

The diagnosis of myocardial infarction is usually made
by the presence of Q _____.

waves

NOTE: The Q wave is the first downward part of the QRS
complex and is never preceded by anything in the complex.
If there is any positive wave — even a tiny spike — in a
QRS complex before the downward wave, we must call it an
S wave (the upward part preceding it was an R wave).

Q waves are _____ in most of the leads in the tracing
of a normal person.

absent

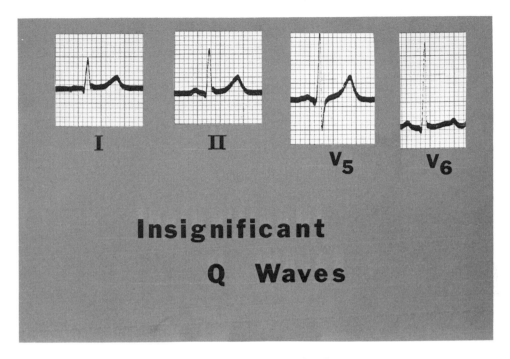

Tiny Q waves may be seen normally in some leads.

Very small Q waves may be present _____ in certain leads.

normally

When these small Q waves are present, they are called _____ Q waves because they do not signify the presence of an infarction.

insignificant

Leads I, II, V₅, and V₆ commonly contain insignificant _____ waves.

Q

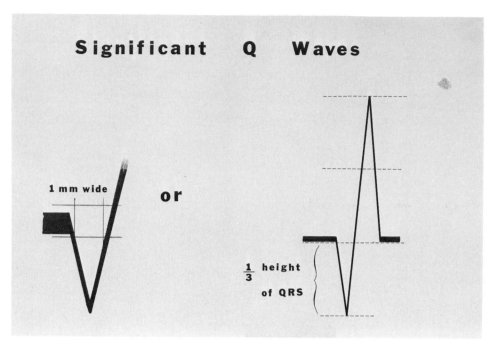

A significant Q wave is one small square wide (.04 sec.) or one-third the size of the QRS complex.

Significant _____ waves are indicative of pathology — namely the presence of an infarction.

Q

A significant Q wave is usually one small square (i.e. one millimeter) wide and is therefore _____ second in duration.

.04

Another helpful standard of a significant Q wave is when the Q wave is one-third the size (height and depth) of the entire _____ complex.

QRS

NOTE: Either of the above criteria are adequate to make the diagnosis.

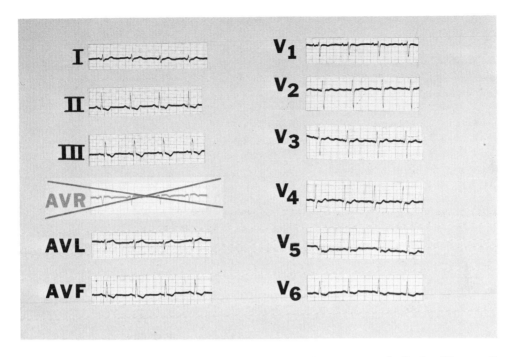

When looking at a tracing, note in which leads you can find significant Q waves. (Omit AVR)

To check for infarction one should scan all the leads for the presence of _____ Q waves.

significant

NOTE: Forget about lead AVR since this lead is positioned such that data regarding Q waves is unreliable. Careful examination will reveal that lead AVR is like an upside-down lead II. So the large Q wave which is commonly seen in AVR is really the upside-down R wave from lead II. Even if you don't understand the logic behind AVR's phony Q's, don't check it for signs of infarction.

When checking a tracing, either on the long strip or mounted, write down exactly which _____ in which you find significant Q waves.

leads

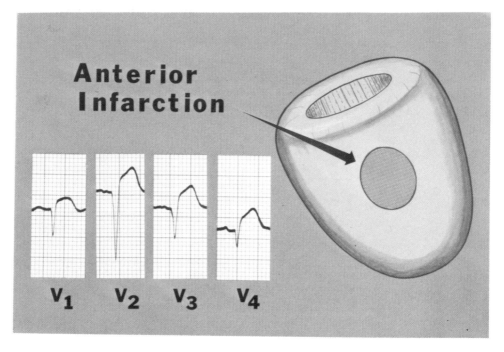

Q waves in V_1, V_2, V_3, V_4 signify an anterior infarction. Is this one acute?

The presence of Q waves in leads V_1, V_2, V_3, or V_4 indicate an infarction in the anterior portion of the _____ ventricle.

left

NOTE: The anterior portion of the left ventricle includes part of the interventricular septum. Some cardiologists says that when Q waves appear in V_1 and V_2, these infarctions include the septum and are therefore often called "septal" infarctions. For all practical purposes, the presence of significant Q waves (remember V_5 and V_6 may have tiny normal Q's) in the chest leads means anterior infarction.

Any anterior infarction may cause significant ____ waves in any of the chest leads or just one chest lead. The chest leads are mainly *anteriorly* placed, and that's a good way to remember how to diagnose *anterior* infarction.

Q

NOTE: Because of the ST elevation, this is an acute anterior infarction.

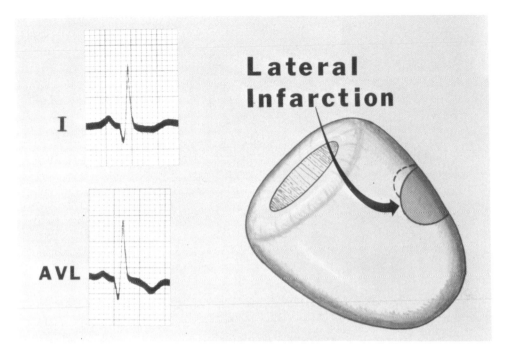

If there arc Q waves in leads I and AVL, there is a lateral infarction.

A lateral infarction is one that has affected the portion of
the _____ ventricle which is closest to the patient's   left
left side.

When a lateral infarction occurs, it will cause Q _____   waves
to appear in leads I and AVL. The one illustrated above
is old.

NOTE: One might abbreviate Lateral Infarction as L.I.
Just remember AV *L* for "Lateral" and "I" for infarction
(after all Roman Numeral I is just a capital i). It's an easy
way to recall the leads demonstrating lateral infarction.

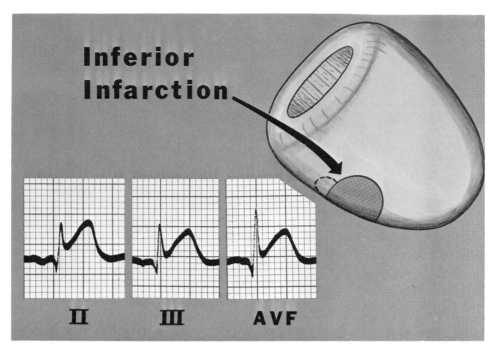

Inferior (diaphragmatic) infarction is designated by Q waves in II, III, and AVF.

The inferior wall of the heart rests upon the diaphragm so the term diaphragmatic infarction refers to an infarction in the inferior portion of the left _____.

ventricle

The _____ infarction is identified by significant Q waves in leads II, III, and AVF.

inferior

NOTE: If I told you the way I remember the leads for inferior infarction this book would be banned. An acute inferior infarction would probably be diagnosed by a person who notices significant Q waves in leads II, III, and AVF, and ST elevation in those leads. Is the one shown above acute?

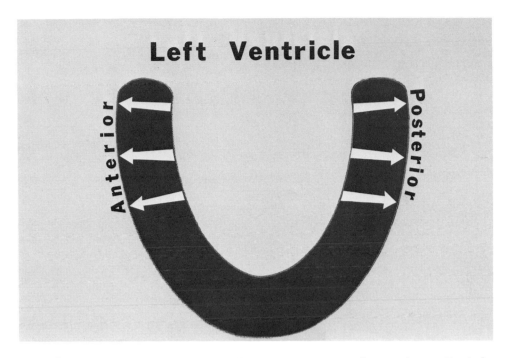

Note that the electrical activity of the anterior area and posterior wall of the left ventricle is in opposite directions.

Depolarization of the anterior wall of the left ventricle
proceeds from the _____ lining of the left ventricle
anteriorly.   inner

Depolarization of the posterior wall of the _____   left
ventricle proceeds from the inner lining of the left ventricle
through the full thickness of the ventricular wall to the
outside or epicardium.

Vectors representing the depolarization of the anterior and
posterior portions of the left ventricle point in
_____ directions.   opposite

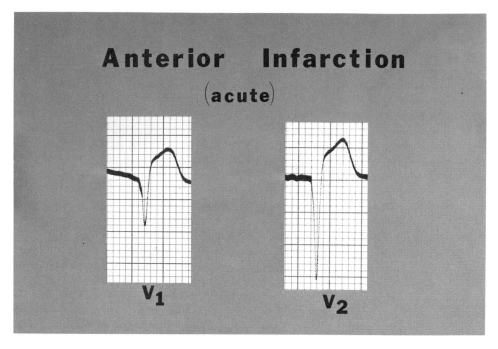

If we see Q waves and ST elevation (in V_1 and V_2) with acute anterior in-farction, a posterior infarction would appear the opposite.

An acute anterior infarction produces significant Q waves in the chest leads with ST _____ in the same leads.　　　　elevation

Just considering V_1 and V_2 the appearance of significant Q waves and ST elevation would be indicative of acute _____ infarction.　　　　anterior

NOTE: Acute posterior infarction of the left ventricle would produce the exact opposite to the pattern of acute anterior infarction because the anterior and posterior walls of the left ventricle depolarize in opposite directions.

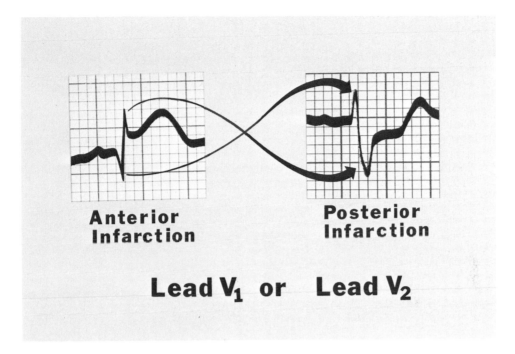

Anterior Infarction

Posterior Infarction

Lead V₁ or Lead V₂

In acute posterior infarction there is a large R wave (the opposite of a Q wave) in V_1 and V_2.

NOTE: In lead V_1, for instance, a Q wave turned upside-down would appear like an R wave (and as you will recall, R waves are usually very tiny in V_1).

A significant "Q wave" from an infarction in the posterior portion of the left _____ will cause a large R (positive deflection) wave in lead V_1.

ventricle

Suspect a true posterior infarction when you see a large _____ wave in V_1 or V_2 even though Right Ventricular Hypertrophy can cause them.

R

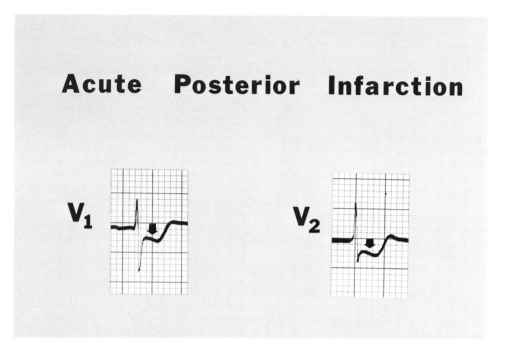

Acute Posterior Infarction

In acute posterior infarction, there will also be ST depression (opposite the "usual" elevation) in V_1 or V_2.

An acute anterior infarction will cause Q waves in the chest leads and the ST segments will be ——————.

elevated

NOTE: Since the posterior wall of the left ventricle depolarizes in a direction opposite to that of the anterior wall, an acute infarct to the posterior wall will cause ST DEPRESSION in V_1 or V_2.

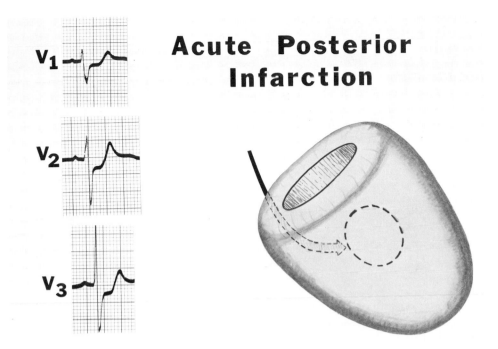

Acute Posterior Infarction

In summary, acute posterior infarction is characterized by a large R wave and ST depression in V_1, V_2, and or V_3.

NOTE: Always be suspicious of ST segment depression in the chest leads — it could indicate a true posterior infarction. (If you do not recall those things which can cause ST depression, look back at page 213). The diagnosis of an anterior subendocardial infarction (because of depressed ST segment in chest leads) should be made with extreme caution because this may really represent an acute true posterior infarct. Occasional reciprocal changes may produce a significant Q wave in V_6.

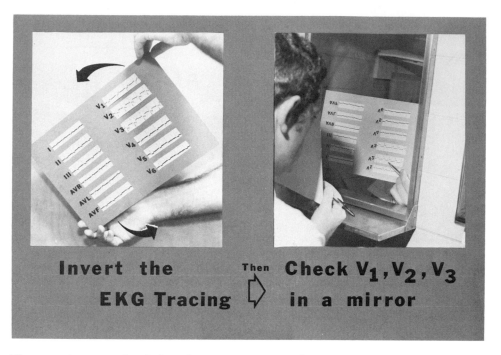

Invert the   Then **Check V₁,V₂,V₃**

EKG Tracing ▷ **in a mirror**

If an acute posterior infarction is suspected (large R and ST depression in V₁ or V₂) try the "mirror test".

NOTE: If a posterior infarction is suspected by tall R waves and ST depression in V₁ or V₂ try the mirror test.
    First, turn the entire tracing upside-down. Then, look at V₁ and V₂ in a mirror and you should see the classical signs of acute infarction, i.e. a big Q wave and ST elevation. Turn back to the previous page and try it. It is an easy maneuver to perform if you can keep from looking at yourself in the mirror.

This test consists of two maneuvers, namely inverting the tracing and looking at the inverted V₁ and V₂ in a _____.   mirror

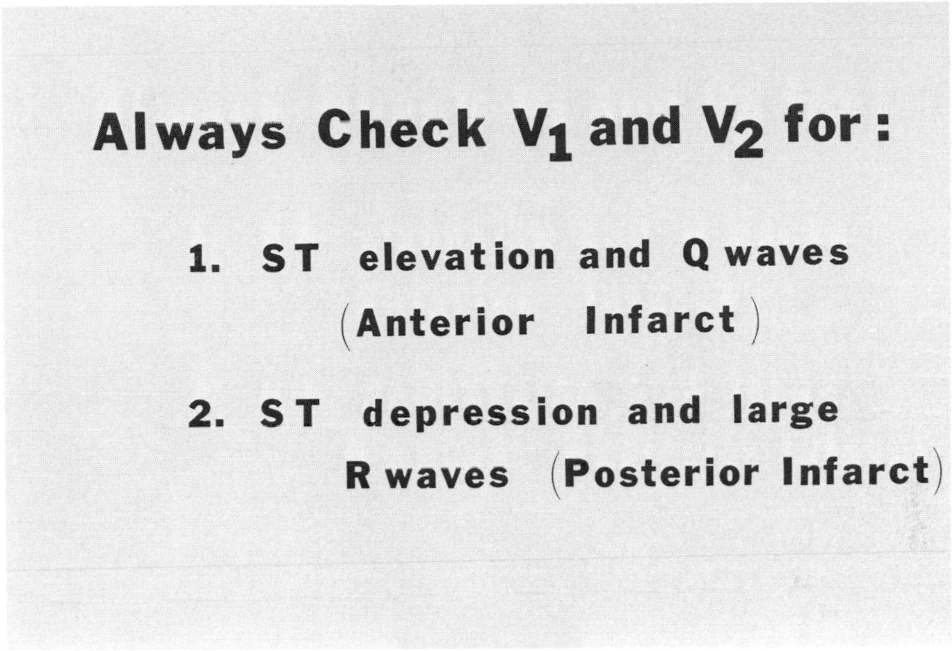

Always Check V₁ and V₂ for:

1. ST elevation and Q waves (Anterior Infarct)

2. ST depression and large R waves (Posterior Infarct)

Although posterior infarctions are very severe they are easy to overlook.

When making your routine reading of an EKG, pay special attention to leads V_1 and _____ while looking for signs of infarction.

V_2

NOTE: ST changes in leads V_1 and V_2 are always significant and important. Both depression *and* elevation.

Check for Q waves in V_1 and V_2 and also observe the height of the _____ waves.

R

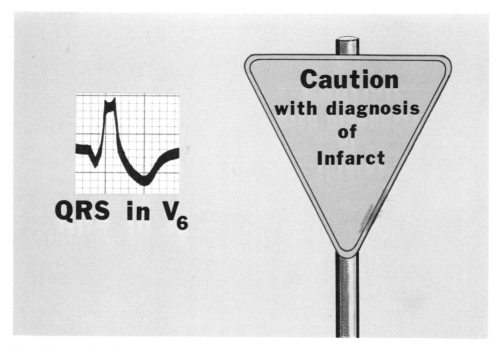

QRS in V₆

Caution
with diagnosis
of
Infarct

The diagnosis of infarction by EKG is generally not valid in the presence of Left Bundle Branch Block.

In Left Bundle Block, the left ventricle (which is the only chamber to infarct) depolarizes after the _____ ventricle.

right

So any Q wave originating from the left ventricle could not appear at the beginning of the QRS _____ (in Left B.B.B.) and would fall somewhere in the middle of the QRS complex. Thus it would be impossible to identify significant Q's in this case.

complex

NOTE: One special exception is possible. The right and left ventricle share the interventricular septum in common. So an infarct in the septal area would be shared by the right ventricle which depolarizes first in Left B.B.B. This would produce Q waves at the beginning of the wide QRS. Therefore even in the presence of the Left B.B.B., Q waves in the chest leads would make one suspect (but not confirm) septal (anterior) infarction.

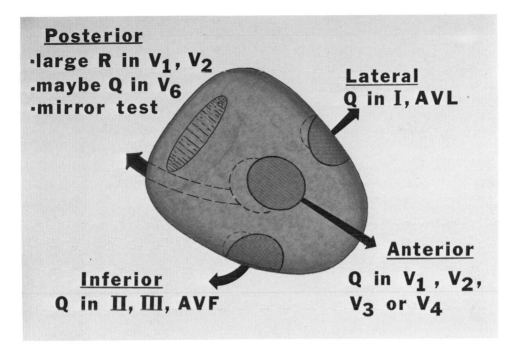

Posterior
- large R in V_1, V_2
- maybe Q in V_6
- mirror test

Lateral
Q in I, AVL

Inferior
Q in II, III, AVF

Anterior
Q in V_1, V_2, V_3 or V_4

Locating an infarct is important because the prognosis depends on the location of the infarction.

There are _____ general locations within the left ventricle where infarctions commonly occur.   four

NOTE: More than one area in the left ventricle may infarct. One area may be very old and one very recent, so correlate the ST elevation with the appropriate leads for the location of an infarct.

Be careful about diagnosing an infarction in the presence of a _____ Bundle Branch Block.   Left

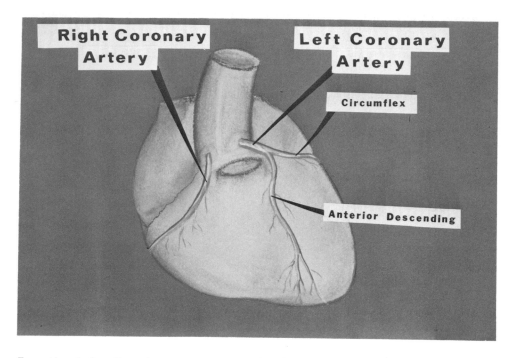

Locating infarctions is a common practice, but with a little anatomical knowledge of the heart's coronary blood supply, we can make a far more sophisti-
cated diagnosis.

There are _____ coronary arteries which   two
provide the heart with a nutrient supply
of oxygenated blood.

The Left coronary artery has two major
branches; they are the Circumflex branch
and the Anterior _____ branch.   Descending

The _____ coronary artery curves around   Right
the right ventricle.

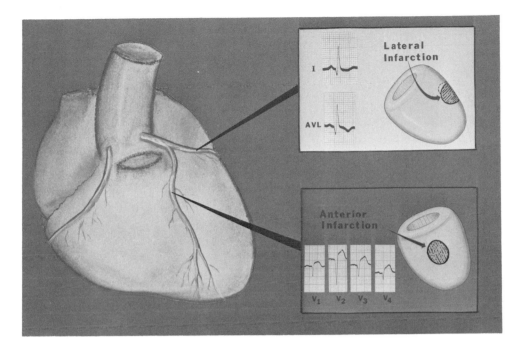

A lateral infarction is caused by an occlusion of the Circumflex branch of the Left coronary artery. An anterior infarction is due to an occlusion of the Anterior Descending branch of the Left coronary artery.

The Circumflex branch of the Left coronary artery distributes blood to the _____ portion of the left ventricle.

lateral

The Anterior Descending branch of the left coronary artery supplies the _____ part of the left ventricle with blood.

anterior

The Circumflex and the Anterior Descending are the two main branches of the _____ coronary artery.

Left

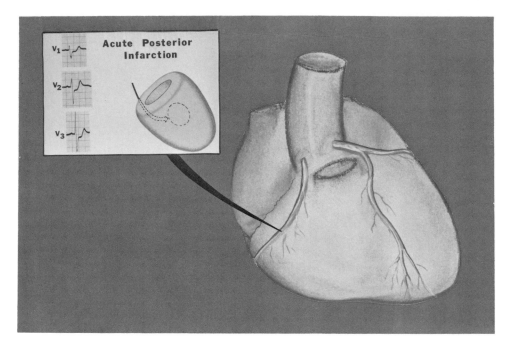

Acute Posterior Infarction

True posterior infarctions are generally due to an occlusion of the Right coronary artery or one of its smaller branches.

The _____ coronary artery swings around behind the right ventricle to supply the posterior portion of the left ventricle.

Right

A posterior infarction is caused by an occlusion of a branch of the Right _____ artery.

coronary

NOTE: For a long time the Right coronary artery was considered to play only a minor role in the blood supply of the heart. The recently perfected technique of coronary angiography has shown that the Right coronary artery provides the local blood supply to the S A Node, A V Node and the (A V) Bundle of His. It is no wonder that acute posterior infarctions are often associated with dangerous arrhythmias. The wisest of cardiologists have always feared and respected the posterior M.I.

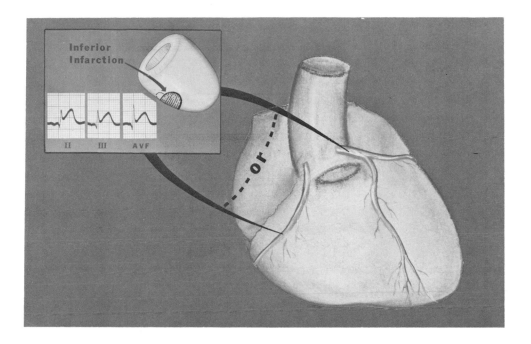

The base of the left ventricle obtains its blood supply from either the right or the left coronary branches, depending on which artery is dominant.

Inferior (or "diaphragmatic") infarctions are caused by an _____ of either the Right or Left coronary artery branches.

occlusion

So the diagnosis of inferior _____ does not identify the artery branch which is occluded unless you have a previous coronary angiogram (an x-ray outlining the coronary arteries) to show which artery supplied the inferior portion of the heart (in that particular patient).

infarction

NOTE: Radiologists define Left or Right coronary "dominance" as denoting which artery renders the greatest portion of blood supply to the base of the left ventricle in a given patient. For instance if the coronary angiogram of a patient demonstrates that his Left coronary artery renders most of the blood supply to the base of the left ventricle, there is a "dominant" Left coronary artery in that patient.

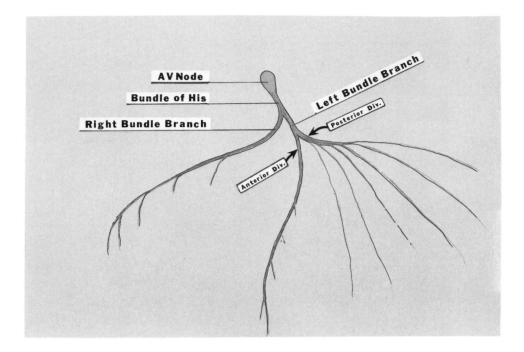

Hemiblocks are presented in this section (Infarction) because they are commonly associated with infarction and a resultant diminished blood supply to the Bundle Branch conduction system.

NOTE: Before proceeding further, please read the first Note on page 245.

The hemiblocks are blocks of the anterior or posterior division of the _____ Bundle Branch.   Left

Hemiblocks are commonly (but not always) due to loss of blood supply to either the Anterior or _____ division of the Left Bundle Branch.   Posterior

NOTE: The Right Bundle Branch does not have significant, recognizable divisions of either clinical or electro-cardiographic importance (yet).

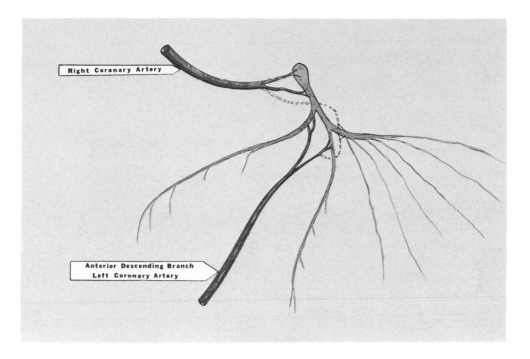

To understand hemiblocks, one must understand the blood supply to the Bundle Branch conduction system of the ventricles (see Note page 232).

The right coronary artery usually renders a blood supply to the A V Node, Bundle of His, and a variable twig to the Posterior division of the Left _____ Branch.

Bundle

The left coronary artery also sends a variable twig of _____ supply to the Posterior division of the Left Bundle Branch.

blood

A total occlusion of the Anterior descending branch of the left coronary artery may cause a subsequent Right Bundle Branch _____ and also an Anterior Hemiblock.

Block

NOTE: The key to understanding Hemiblocks is to keep in mind that an infarction may be due to an occlusion of a vessel at various locations or levels and may cause any variety of blocks of the Bundle Branch system i.e. single blocks of one bundle or division or combinations of these blocks sparing one or more branches.

Anterior Hemiblock

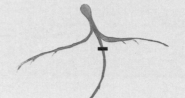

- L.A.D. - usually assoc. with an M.I. (or other heart disease)

- QRS slightly widened (.10 to .12)

- $Q_1 S_3$

Anterior Hemiblock refers to a block of the anterior division of the Left Bundle Branch and the above criteria are used in the diagnosis.

The slight delay of conduction to the anterior, lateral and superior area of the left ventricle causes (late) unopposed depolarization upward to the left recognized as Left _____ Deviation.

Axis

With pure Anterior Hemiblock, the QRS is widened only .10 to .12 sec., but association with other blocks of the _____ Branch system may widen the QRS more.

Bundle

Anterior Hemiblock is usually noted to cause a Q in I and a wide and/or deep _____ in III ($Q_1 S_3$).

S

NOTE: Previous tracings are essential in making Anterior (or any) Hemiblock diagnosis. You *must* always rule out pre-existing sources of Left Axis Deviation, e.g. Left Ventricular Hypertrophy, Horizontal Heart, or Inferior Infarction.

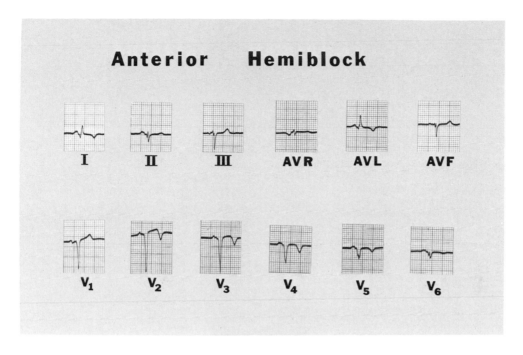

Probably one-half of patients with Anterior Infarctions also develop Anterior Hemiblock.

Anterior Hemiblock describes a block of the Anterior Division of the Left Bundle Branch causing a delay in depolarization to that (anterior, lateral, and superior) area of the left _____,   ventricle to produce Left Axis Deviation.

Anterior _____ can cause Anterior Hemiblock (that's   infarctions easy to remember).

A patient with an abnormal QRS Vector of $-60°$ for ten years has a difficult EKG for determining Anterior _____.   Hemiblock

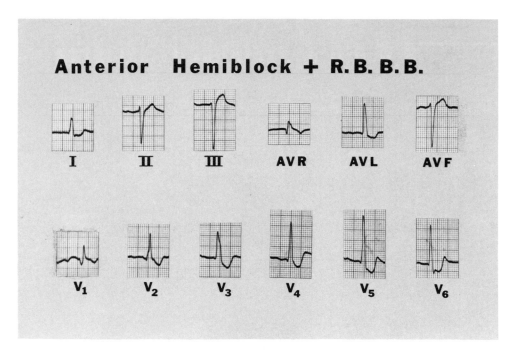

Anterior Hemiblock + R.B.B.B.

An infarction of the anterior wall of the left ventricle (due to occlusion of the Anterior Descending branch of the left coronary artery) may cause Anterior Hemiblock (and R.B.B.B.).

NOTE: Don't forget that the Anterior Descending Artery also renders blood supply to the Right Bundle Branch, so Anterior Infarction may have an associated R.B.B.B. depending on the level of occlusion.

A patient with a previously normal QRS Axis has an Anterior myocardial infarction and a subsequent QRS axis of -40°.
He probably has an Anterior _____.

Hemiblock

A patient with an Inferior Infarction develops Left Axis Deviation. Beware! Inferior Infarction can cause L.A.D. so _____ Hemiblock is not the prime suspect.

Anterior

Posterior Hemiblock

- **R.A.D. - usually assoc. with an M.I. (or other heart disease)**

- **Normal or slightly widened QRS**

- **$S_1 Q_3$**

Pure isolated Posterior Hemiblock is rare because the posterior division is short, thick, and commonly has a dual blood supply.

An inferior infarction may destroy the blood supply to the Posterior division of the Left Bundle _____.   Branch

Look for a deep or unusually wide S in I and Q in III known as $S_1 Q_3$ when _____ Hemiblock is suspected.   Posterior

Posterior Hemiblocks cause _____ Axis deviation due to the late, unopposed depolarization forces toward the right.   Right

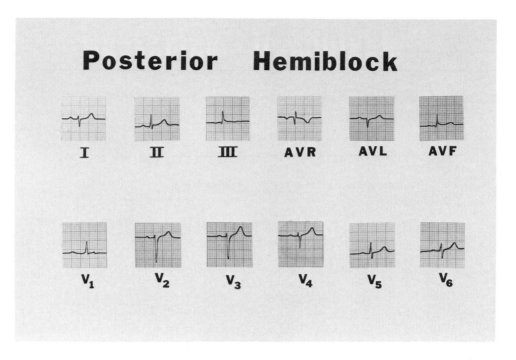

Posterior Hemiblock is always to be respected, and all Inferior Infarctions should be scrutinized to rule it out.

A lateral infarction either recent or old may produce
Right Axis _____ which can be confused with Posterior   Deviation
Hemiblock. It is said that in the presence of lateral M.I.,
the EKG diagnosis of Posterior Hemiblock is avoided.

Make certain that by history and previous EKG's _____   Right
Axis Deviation due to slender body build, Right
Ventricular Hypertrophy, pulmonary disease etc. is
ruled out.

Posterior _____ are serious, and when in association   Hemiblocks
with Right Bundle Branch Block, they are considered very
dangerous because of the predisposition of progression
into A V Blocks.

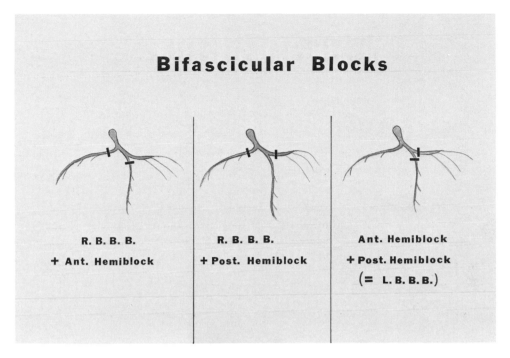

Bifascicular Blocks

R. B. B. B.

+ Ant. Hemiblock

R. B. B. B.

+ Post. Hemiblock

Ant. Hemiblock

+ Post. Hemiblock

(= L. B. B. B.)

Fascicle means bundle so any division of the Ventricular conduction system is a fascicle.

NOTE: For many years "Bundle" referred to either the Right or Left Bundle Branch. When referring to combinations of blocks (e.g. Hemiblock + Bundle Branch Block) we use the word fascicular block to imply a bundle branch block and a hemiblock. (fascicle means bundle literally).

NOTE: Bifascicular block means *two* fascicles are blocked. Because Anterior Hemiblock plus Posterior Hemiblock is generally indistinguishable from Left Bundle Branch Block, Bifascicular Block generally refers to Right Bundle Branch Block together with a block of either the Anterior Division or the Posterior Division of the Left Bundle Branch.

Intermittent Blocks
...with at least one normal, non-blocked fascicle

Intermittent block of one fascicle: continuous EKG pattern of normal with intermittent signs of block.

Intermittent block of two fascicles: intermittent EKG signs of both blocks.

Intermittent block:
one intermittent + one permanent block
... continuous EKG pattern of one block
and intermittent signs of another block.

Fortunately, combinations of [fascicular] blocks are often intermittent, so that when in combination with other blocks they are more easily recognized and treated.

A patient with a block of one or more fascicles may have an associated intermittent _____ of another fascicle producing intermittent (or occasional) signs of block of another fascicle.

block

A patient may have a permanent fascicular block and an intermittent block in one or more of the other _____.

fascicles

Intermittent block may exist in more than one fascicle in the same patient at once, producing intermittent _____ signs (as varying QRS axis).

EKG

NOTE: Like a loose light bulb which occasionally (intermittently) does not light, fascicles may suffer intermittent block. However, unlike loose light bulbs, intermittent fascicular blocks often warn of impending permanent block of that fascicle. When permanent blocks of other fascicles already exist, intermittent fascicular block is a warning to the clinician that a pacemaker may be necessary (see next page). That is why the first printed word in this page is "Fortunately".

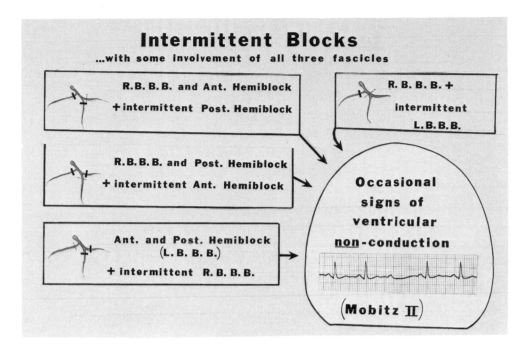

Intermittent Blocks
...with some involvement of all three fascicles

R.B.B.B. and Ant. Hemiblock

+intermittent Post. Hemiblock

R.B.B.B. +

intermittent

L.B.B.B.

R.B.B.B. and Post. Hemiblock

+ intermittent Ant. Hemiblock

Ant. and Post. Hemiblock
(L.B.B.B.)

+ intermittent R.B.B.B.

Occasional
signs of
ventricular
non-conduction

(Mobitz II)

Considering the three pathways of ventricular depolarization, it becomes apparent that one [fascicle] must remain open at least intermittently to provide ventricular conduction.

Trifascicular blocks are diagnosed only when one or more of the fascicular _____ is intermittent.

blocks

"Bilateral" (left and right) Bundle _____ Block diagnosis, similarly, is made only if the block is intermittent in one or both of the bundles.

Branch

Complete, permanent Trifascicular block or Bilateral Bundle Branch Block is indistinguishable from complete (3°) AV _____.

Block

NOTE: If all fascicles are permanently blocked except one which is intermittently blocked, a Mobitz II type pattern (i.e. occasional non-conduction to ventricles) is noted. So the appearance of Mobitz II patterns carries much weight for a decision to implant a pacemaker.

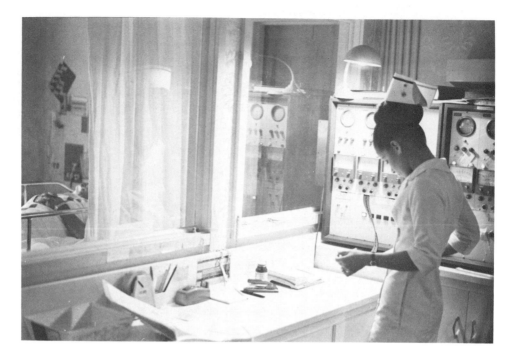

In many hospitals, patients with acute myocardial infarctions are placed in coronary care units and monitored continuously. In some hospitals all patients with suspected infarctions are placed in such units.

NOTE: Just as the preferred treatment of various arrhythmias changes with the times, so the attitudes toward indications for implantation of artificial pacemakers is constantly changing relative to A V Blocks, Bundle Branch and fascicular blocks, intermittent blocks etc. Therefore it is essential that you keep up with the current medical literature.

The subject of severity of infarction relative to its position in the left _____ is very controversial, so each one of us must be well read on the subject to make our own decisions.

ventricle

NOTE: Infarctions may "extend" or progressively involve a larger area of the left ventricle. Obviously, extension of acute infarctions carries a less favorable prognosis than the original infarct.

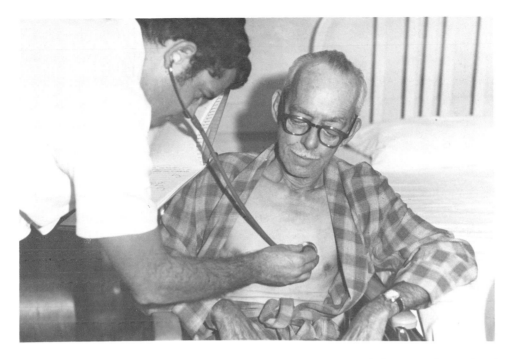

Remember that the clinical diagnosis and history are still the most important standards of the diagnosis of acute infarction.

The EKG has been called "only an aid" in the diagnosis of myocardial _____ even though it probably gives more specific information than any other parameter.

infarction

There is no substitute for taking and evaluating a thorough _____.

history

The laboratory also gives us many ways to evaluate the status of the patient, but careful _____ interpretation is essential.

EKG

NOTE: The electrocardiogram is a useful diagnostic aid, but its value increases multifold when compared to a patient's previous tracings. Always attempt to obtain a patient's previous EKG's for comparison, because electrocardiograms like x-rays become much more valuable when we can be certain that pathology is recent or old.

NOTE: Review Infarction by turning to the small notebook sheets at the end of this book (pages 274-275).

Miscellaneous Effects

- **Pulmonary**

- **Electrolytes**

- **Patterns**

- **Drugs**

The above effects can produce changes in the electrocardiogram which are common to, but not diagnostic of, certain conditions.

NOTE: These following effects may be recognized by a characteristic appearance on electrocardiogram. For most of the conditions mentioned in this section, these electrocardiographic signs merely make one suspicious of certain pathology, or drug or electrolyte effects. In these cases one would obtain further diagnostic tests to confirm the suspicion. Rarely is a diagnosis made entirely on the existence of any of the following EKG findings.

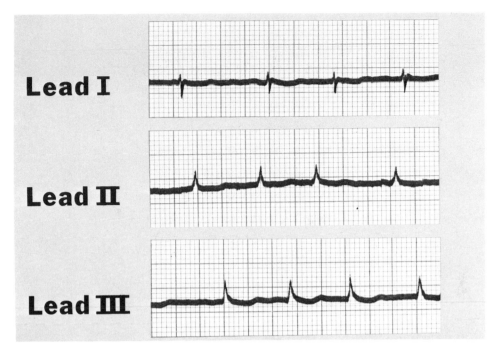

Emphysema usually produces low voltage in all leads and there is often Right Axis Deviation.

Severe _____ commonly produces QRS complexes of small amplitude in all leads. Indeed, this pulmonary disease diminishes the voltage (deflection) of all waves.

emphysema

Due to pulmonary emphysema the right ventricle is working against resistance; this may cause _____ Axis Deviation.

Right

The Right Axis Deviation is usually due to Right Ventricular Hypertrophy. We can diagnose Right Axis Deviation by simply noting that the _____ in lead I is mainly negative.

QRS

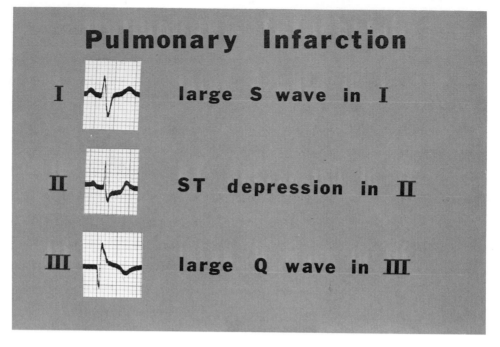

With Pulmonary Infarction we may see a large S wave in lead I, and a Q wave in III. ST depression is usually present in lead II.

S_1 Q_3 syndrome characterizes acute cor pulmonale as a result of pulmonary infarction. It is called S_1 Q_3 because of the large S wave in lead I and the significant _____ wave in III.

Q

NOTE: Observe the tendency toward Right Axis Deviation (lead I).

There is also usually ST _____ in lead II.

depression

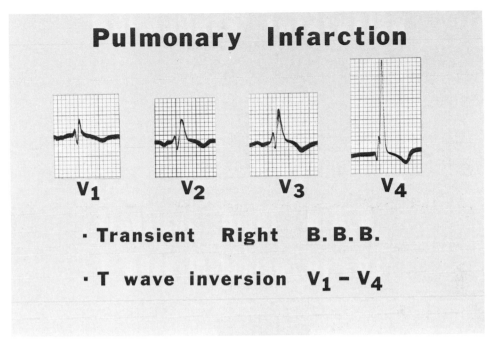

Pulmonary Infarction

V_1　　V_2　　V_3　　V_4

· Transient Right B.B.B.

· T wave inversion V_1 - V_4

With Pulmonary Infarction there is commonly T wave inversion in V_1 through V_4. There is often Right Bundle Branch Block.

_____ wave inversion in the chest leads, particularly lead V_1 through V_4, is a very important diagnostic sign of pulmonary infarction.

T

Pulmonary _____ may cause Right Bundle Branch Block. This block usually subsides after the patient improves.

infarction

We can recognize the presence of Right Bundle Branch Block by the R — R′ in the _____ chest leads.

right

NOTE: Occasionally the Right B.B.B. may be "incomplete" (QRS complex of normal width, but R — R′ is present.)

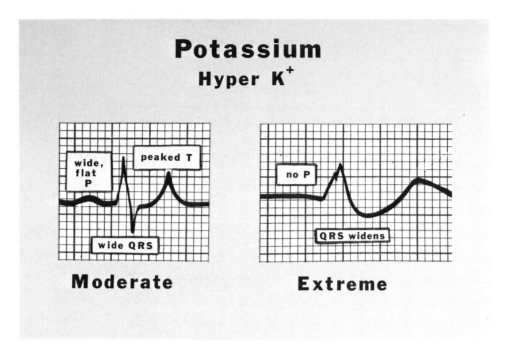

With elevated serum potassium the P wave flattens down, the QRS complex widens, and the T wave becomes peaked.

With an elevated serum potassium, the T wave becomes _____.

peaked

The P wave will flatten down until it is difficult to find in extreme _____.

hyperkalemia

When a patient has an elevated potassium, ventricular depolarization takes longer, and the QRS complex subsequently _____.

widens

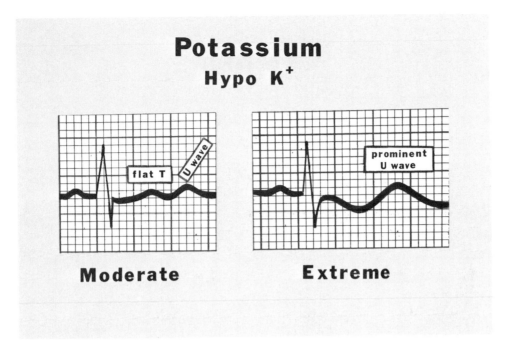

As the serum potassium drops below normal, the T wave becomes flat (or inverted) and there is a U wave.

With low serum potassium, the T wave becomes flat as the _____ drops. As the potassium level becomes lower the T wave may become inverted.

potassium

NOTE: I always think of the T wave as a tent housing potassium ions. As the potassium ions fall below normal, the T wave flattens down. Conversely, increased potassium ions will peak the T wave upward.

With hypokalemia a _____ wave appears. This wave becomes more prominent as the loss of potassium becomes more severe.

U

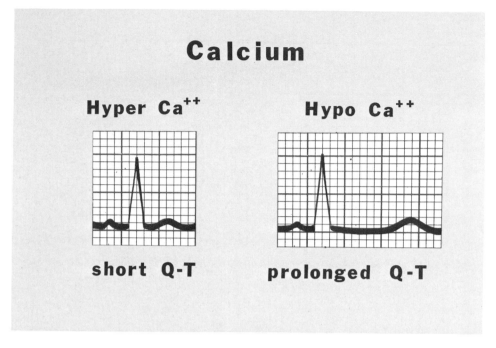

With hypercalcemia the Q-T interval shortens, but with hypocalcemia the Q-T interval becomes prolonged.

Hypocalcemia will usually _____ the Q-T interval.

prolong

NOTE: The Q-T interval is measured from the beginning of the Q wave to the *end* of the T wave.

Increased serum Calcium apparently enhances early ventricular repolarization (after depolarization). This produces a short _____ interval.

Q-T

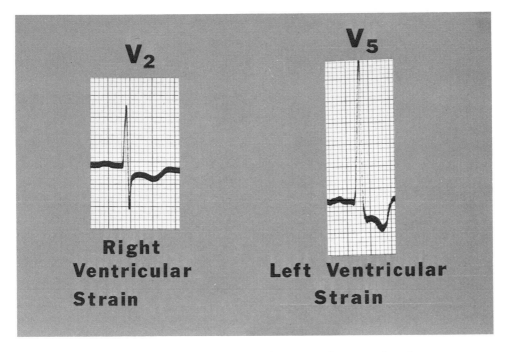

With ventricular strain the ST segment becomes depressed and wavy.

Ventricular strain is characterized by moderate depression
of the _____ segment.

ST

NOTE: Strain is often associated with ventricular
hypertrophy which is logical since a ventricle which is
straining against some kind of resistance (e.g. valvular or
increased vascular resistance) will become hypertrophied
in attempt to compensate.

Ventricular _____ causes a depressed ST segment
which generally curves upward or humps gradually in the
middle of the segment.

strain

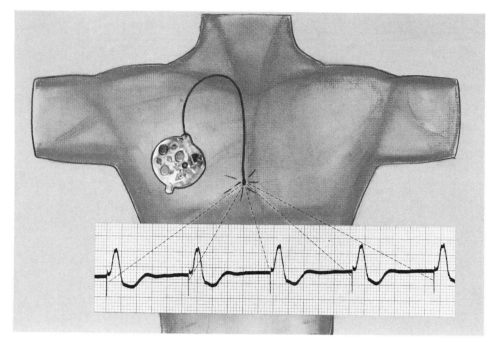

An artificial (battery operated) pacemaker produces electrical spikes. Immediately after each spike we expect to see a ventricular response.

NOTE: Artificial pacemakers are surgically implanted in patients with third degree A V Block. In this complete block the ventricular rate is so slow (30-40/min.) that a battery operated pacemaker is needed to keep the heart pumping at a normal rate. The battery portion is implanted under the skin and the wire leads are either passed through the venous system into the right ventricle ("transvenous"), or the electrodes are sewn into the outside of the ventricular wall ("epicardial").

The pacemaker emits an _____ impulse regularly, producing a small vertical spike on EKG.

electrical

We expect each impulse to "capture" (i.e. depolarize) the ventricles. Because this artificial ventricular depolarization is "ectopic" each response will look like a _____.

P.V.C.

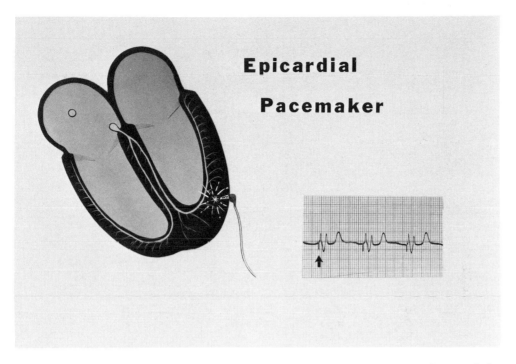

By examination of the EKG, one can determine the type of pacemaker and the location of the (stimulating) catheter tip.

Epicardial pacemakers are located on the epicardial surface on the left _____ so the left ventricle depolarizes before the right and   ventricle

...this produces a QRS with a Right Bundle _____ Block pattern.   Branch

Epicardial pacemakers produce a QRS with a _____ Bundle Branch Block pattern and usually right axis deviation as well.   Right

Right Ventricular Pacemakers
(all have L.B.B.B. pattern QRS)

If L.A.D. → pacemaker in apex of R. Ventricle

If Normal Axis → R. Ventricular mid-outflow tract

If R.A.D. → R. Ventricle, below pulmonic valves

Right Ventricular pacemakers are the most common type, the catheter tip is within the cavity of the right ventricle.

NOTE: The most ideal location for a Right Ventricular [transvenous] pacemaker is to have the catheter tip at the apex of the right ventricular cavity. The resultant QRS has a L.B.B.B. pattern and Left Axis Deviation.

When a paced QRS shows a L.B.B.B. _____ with a normal axis, the catheter tip is in the Right Ventricular mid-out flow tract.   pattern

But if there is a paced QRS with a L.B.B.B. pattern and Right Axis Deviation, the _____ tip is below the pulmonic valves.   catheter

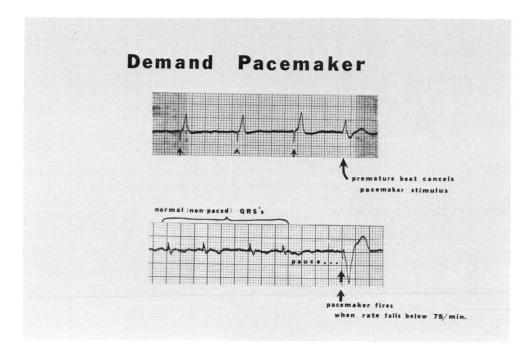

The "demand" pacemaker has input sensing ability, a ready pacemaker stimulus, and a "brain" to determine when to pace and when to stop.

The demand pacemaker will fire on "demand" when it
senses a _____ in rate below a predetermined level.   decrease

... and should the rate return (to normal), the
demand _____ will sense the normal rhythm and shut   pacemaker
itself off so it will not compete with the normal rhythm.

The _____ pacemaker can sense a P.V.C. so that the   demand
next pacemaker stimulus begins after an interval similar
to the usual interval between paced beats.

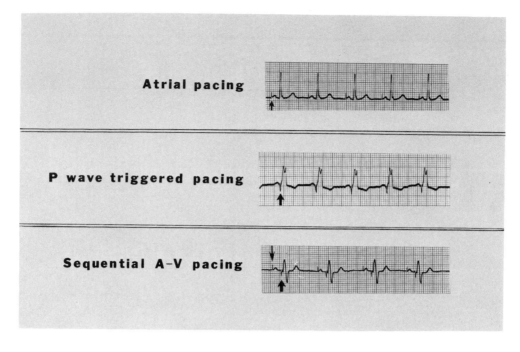

It is well to recognize other types of pacing even though their use is uncommon.

In atrial pacing, the pacemaker stimulates the _____ and conduction proceeds normally in the remainder of each cycle.

atria

However, in P wave triggered pacing, the pacemaker unit senses the P wave and then fires a (ventricular) _____ shortly thereafter. (This is also called "atrial synchronous" pacing).

stimulus

In sequential A-V pacing, both the atria and ventricles are stimulated. The first spike depolarizes the atria and after a brief interval the _____ are stimulated by a separate catheter tip.

ventricles

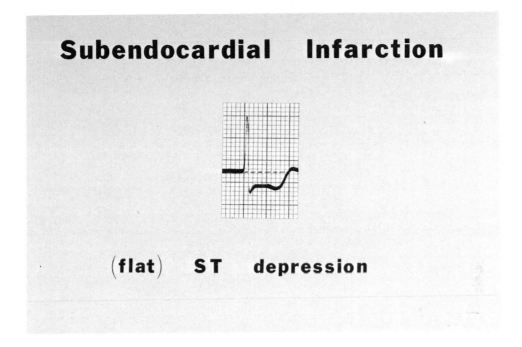

Subendocardial infarction causes flat (horizontal) depression of the ST segment.

Subendocardial infarction (it was originally called subendocardial injury) is identified by ST depression in which the ST _____ remains flat.

segment

NOTE: Subendocardial infarction involves only a small area of myocardium just below the endocardial lining. True myocardial infarctions usually involve the full thickness of (left) ventricular wall in the area which is affected. Even though subendocardial infarctions may involve only small areas of myocardial tissue, they should be treated much like a true M.I. Be cautious because subendocardial infarction is often considered a sign of impending myocardial infarction.

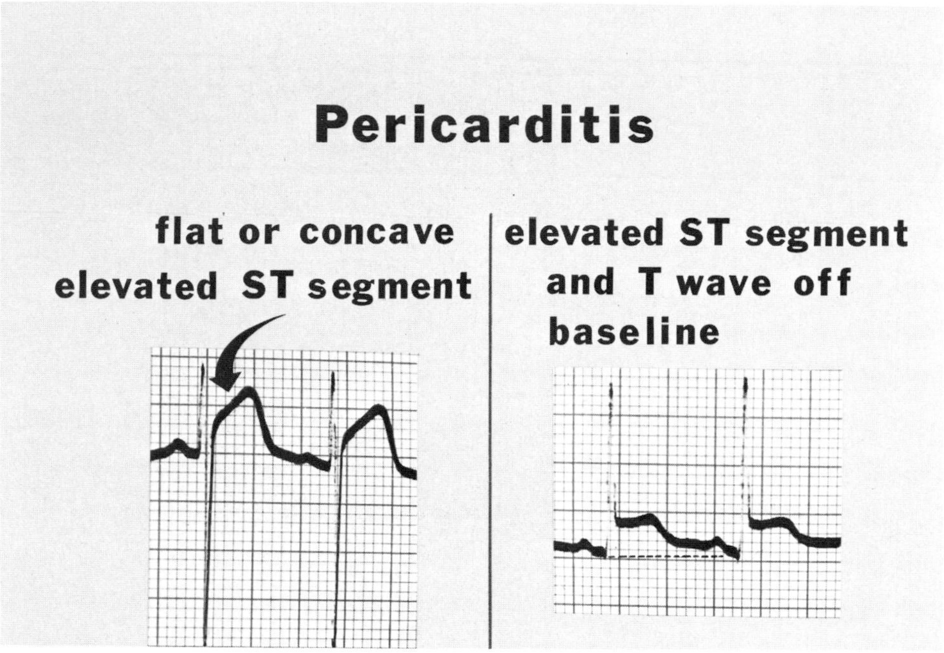

Pericarditis

flat or concave elevated ST segment

elevated ST segment and T wave off baseline

With pericarditis the ST segment is elevated and it is usually flat or concave. The entire T wave may be elevated off the baseline.

Pericarditis can _____ the ST segment. It will usually produce an ST segment which is flat or concave (downwards).

elevate

_____ seems to elevate the entire T wave off the baseline, that is, the baseline angles back down to the P wave of the next cycle.

Pericarditis

NOTE: The characteristics shown in the left hand illustration are found in a lead in which the QRS is usually mainly negative (like the right chest leads). The pattern shown on the right hand illustration is seen in a lead where the QRS is mainly positive (like I or II).

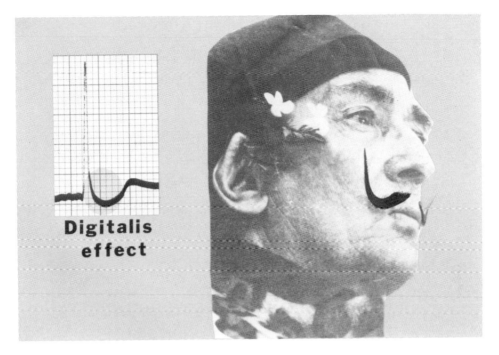

Digitalis causes gradual downward sloping of the ST segment to give it the appearance of Salvador Dali's mustache.

Digitalis produces a unique gradual sloping of the
_____ segment.

ST

NOTE: Find a lead with no demonstrable S wave
to identify this classic pattern. The downward portion of the
R wave gradually becomes thicker as it approaches the
baseline. The downward limb of the R wave has a gentle
curving, downward slope as it blends into the baseline. Note
that the ST segment is slightly depressed as it sags downward.
This pattern can be demonstrated on the EKG of most
digitalized patients.

Excess Digitalis

· **S A Block**

· **P. A. T. with Block**

· **A V Blocks**

· **Tachycardia with A V dissociation**

Excess digitalis tends to cause A V Blocks of many varieties and may cause S A Block.

Digitalis in excess amounts will retard conduction of the atrial stimulus to the A V _____.

Node

_____ digitalis may cause various types of A V Block and tachycardia associated with A V Block.

Excess

NOTE: Always be aware of the fact that digitalis excess is exaggerated by low serum potassium.

Digitalis Toxicity

- P.V.C.'s
- Bigeminy, Trigeminy, etc.
- Ventricular Tachycardia
- Ventricular Fibrillation
- Atrial Fibrillation

Digitalis in toxic amounts will stimulate ectopic ventricular foci to discharge and cause subsequent arrhythmias.

Digitalis in _____ amounts can create irritable ectopic foci particularly in the ventricles.

toxic

Dangerous arrhythmias may arise from ventricular ectopic _____ discharging often or even firing repetitively at a tachycardia rate.

foci

NOTE: Digitalis preparations have been the physician's friend in treating cardiac failure since the thirteenth century. It must be respected, however, because in toxic amounts it can cause deadly arrhythmias.

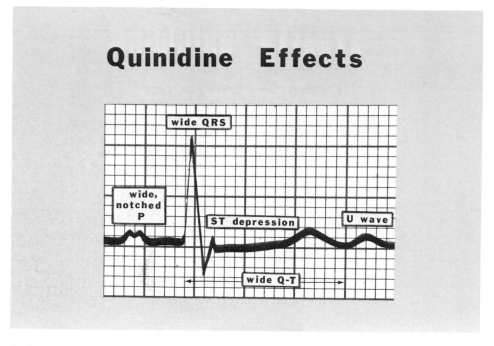

Quinidine Effects

wide QRS

wide, notched P

ST depression

U wave

wide Q-T

Quinidine causes notching of a wide P wave and widening of the QRS complex. There is often ST depression, a prolonged Q-T and U waves.

NOTE: Quinidine retards electrical conduction through the myocardium. Most of the effects of quinidine noted on EKG are related to a slowing of the speed of depolarization and repolarization.

Quinidine causes a wide, notched _____ wave on EKG and also widens the QRS complex.

P

Quinidine can prolong the _____ interval, and depress the ST segment. Look for U waves.

Q-T

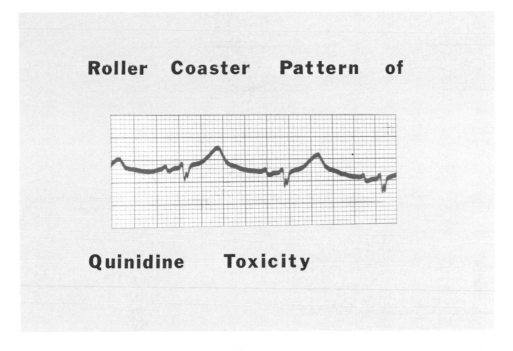

Roller Coaster Pattern of

Quinidine   Toxicity

The roller coaster pattern of quinidine toxicity results from an exaggeration of the effects mentioned on the previous page.

Quinidine in the above tracing has widened the
_____ complex.   QRS

Although the P wave is biphasic in this lead, it was
_____ in lead I and II.   notched

NOTE: Review Miscellaneous by turning to the notebook sheets which begin on the next page.

These notebook sheets are for you to cut out and carry for easy reference (if you own this book).

SEQUENTIAL SCHEME FOR RAPID EKG INTERPRETATION

○ 1. <u>RATE</u>: "300, 150, 100 ... 75, 60, 50"
   a. for bradycardia-
      rate = Cycles/6 sec. strip X 10

○ 2. <u>RHYTHM</u>: Scan tracing for abnormal waves, pauses, and irregularity.
   a. Check for P before each QRS
   b. Check for QRS after each P
○   c. Measure P-R interval
   d. Measure QRS interval

   3. <u>AXIS</u>: QRS above or below the baseline in the following leads-
   a. I, AVF for Normal vs
      R. or L. axis deviation
○   b. "3-D" location I, AVF, and V_2

   4. <u>HYPERTROPHY</u>: Check-
        ⎧ P wave for atrial hypertrophy
○ in V_1 ⎨ R wave for R. Ventric. Hypert.
        ⎩ S wave for L. Ventric. Hypert.
      ... + R wave in V_5 for L.V.H.

○ 5. <u>INFARCTION</u>: Scan all leads for-
   a. Q waves
   b. Inverted T waves
   c. Elevated ST segments

Dubin's
Rapid Method
For
reading E K G 's
1. Rate

A.   Memorize:

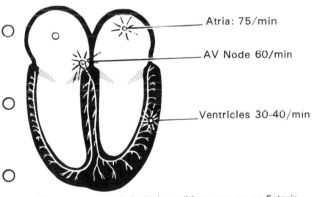

B.   Slow Rates:
        Cycles/6 sec. Strip X 10 = Rate
C.   Always check to see if there are separate atrial (P wave)
        and ventricular (QRS) rates.
D.   Normal Rhythm
        rate more than 100/min. = Sinus Tachycardia
        rate less than 60/min. = Sinus Bradycardia
E.   Inherent Rates (Ectopic Pacemakers)

Atria: 75/min

AV Node 60/min

Ventricles 30-40/min

*Emergency or pathological conditions may cause Ectopic
Focus in Atrium, AV Node, or Ventricle to fire at a Tachycardia rate of 150-250/minute.

2. Rhythm (Always measure P-R interval / Always measure QRS complex)

A. Varying Rhythm

Sinus Arrhythmia
Irregular rhythm. Identical P waves. May indicate coronary disease.

Wandering Pacemaker
Irregular rhythm. P waves change shape as pacemaker location varies.

Atrial Fibrillation
Irregular rhythm. No discernable P waves, but multiple ectopic atrial spikes.

B. Extra Beats and Skips

Premature Beats:
Atrial Premature — ectopic atrial focus fires early P wave; normal QRS follows.

Nodal Premature — ectopic focus in AV node causes early QRS not preceded by a P.

C. Rapid Rhythms
Paroxysmal (sudden) *Tachycardia:*

- *Atrial* — normal wave sequence at rate of 150-250; P wave may not appear.

- *Nodal* — originates in the AV node, so there are no P waves; rate 150-250.

- *Ventricular* — looks like a rapid sequence of P.V.C.'s; rate usually 150-250.

Atrial Flutter — continuous rapid succession of identical P waves.

Ventricular Flutter — smooth diphasic waves like a series of sine wave undulations.

Atrial Fibrillation — multiple ectopic atrial spikes make jagged baseline.

Ventricular Fibrillation — totally erratic electrical activity is deadly.

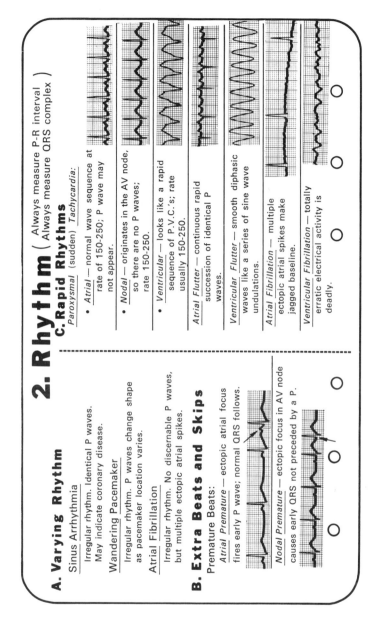

270

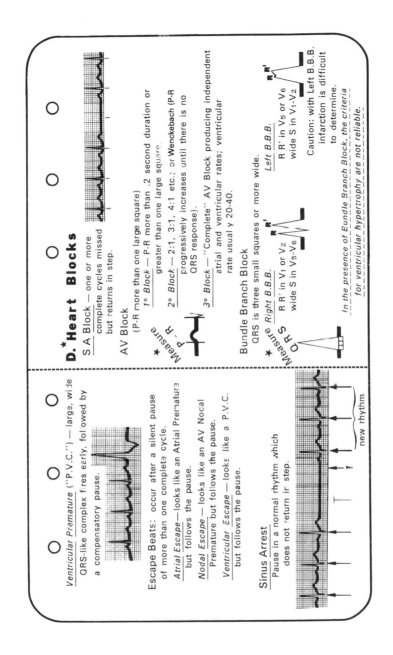

Ventricular Premature ("P.V.C.") — large, wide QRS-like complex fires early, followed by a compensatory pause.

Escape Beats: occur after a silent pause of more than one complete cycle.

Atrial Escape—looks like an Atrial Premature but follows the pause.

Nodal Escape—looks like an AV Nodal Premature but follows the pause.

Ventricular Escape—looks like a P.V.C. but follows the pause.

Sinus Arrest

Pause in a normal rhythm which does not return ir step.

new rhythm

D. *Heart Blocks

S A Block — one or more complete cycles missed but returns in step.

AV Block

(P-R more than one large square)

1° *Block* — P-R more than .2 second duration or greater than one large square.

2° *Block* — 2:1, 3:1, 4:1 etc.; or **Wenckebach** (P-R progressively increases until there is no QRS response).

3° *Block* — "Complete" AV Block producing independent atrial and ventricular rates; ventricular rate usual y 20-40.

Measure P-R

Bundle Branch Block

QRS is three small squares or more wide.

Measure QRS

Right B.B.B.
R R' in V1 or V2
wide S in V5-V6

Left B.B.B.
R R' in V5 or V6
wide S in V1-V2

Caution: with Left B.B.B. infarction is difficult to determine.

In the presence of Bundle Branch Block, the criteria for ventricular hypertrophy are not reliable.

3. Axis

Check Lead I First

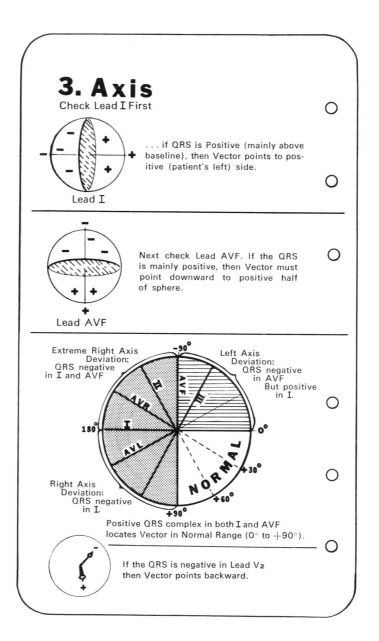

. . . if QRS is Positive (mainly above baseline), then Vector points to positive (patient's left) side.

Lead I

Next check Lead AVF. If the QRS is mainly positive, then Vector must point downward to positive half of sphere.

Lead AVF

Extreme Right Axis Deviation: QRS negative in I and AVF

Left Axis Deviation: QRS negative in AVF But positive in I.

Right Axis Deviation: QRS negative in I.

Positive QRS complex in both I and AVF locates Vector in Normal Range (0° to +90°).

If the QRS is negative in Lead V₂ then Vector points backward.

4. Hypertrophy

1. Atrial Hypertrophy: P wave more than 3 small squares wide $\left[> .12 \text{ sec. wide} \right]$.

$\bigcirc$ **V₁**

A. <u>Right</u> <u>Atrial</u> <u>Hypertrophy</u>
...large, diphasic P wave with tall initial component.

B. <u>Left</u> <u>Atrial</u> <u>Hypertrophy</u>
...large, diphasic P wave with wide terminal componant.

2. Ventricular Hypertrophy

A. <u>Right</u> <u>Ventricular</u> <u>Hypertrophy</u>
· R wave greater than S wave in V₁.
· R wave gets progressively smaller from V₁ to V₆.
· S wave persists in V₅ and V₆.
· Wide QRS.

B. <u>Left</u> <u>Ventricular</u> <u>Hypertrophy</u>
· S wave in V₁ **+** R wave in V₅ add up to more than 35mm.
· Left axis deviation.
· Wide QRS.
· T wave slants down slowly and returns up rapidly (inverted).

5. Infarction

1. Injury = Elevated ST segment

elevation

- Signifies an acute process, ST returns to baseline with time.
- If T wave is also elevated off baseline, suspect pericarditis.
- Location of Injury may be determined like infarction location.
- If ST depression: digitalis or Subendocardial Infarction or Positive Master Test

2. Infarction = Q wave

Q

- Small Q's may be normal in V_5 and V_6.
- To be abnormal Q must be one small square (.04 sec.) wide.
- Also abnormal if Q wave depth is greater than $\frac{1}{3}$ of QRS height in lead III.

3. Ischemia = inverted T wave

T

- Inverted T wave is symmetrical.
- T waves are usually upright in leads I, II, and V_2 - V_6, so check these leads for T wave Inversion.

infarction location
(Left Ventricle)

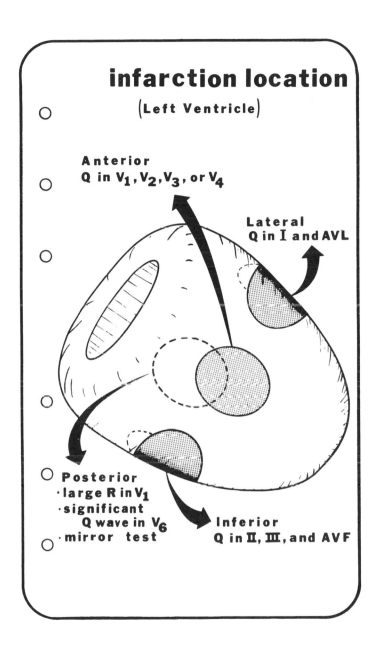

Anterior
Q in V_1, V_2, V_3, or V_4

Lateral
Q in I and AVL

Posterior
· large R in V_1
· significant
  Q wave in V_6
· mirror test

Inferior
Q in II, III, and AVF

Miscellaneous

1. Pulmonary Effects

    A. Emphysema: low voltage in all leads.

    B. Pulmonary Infarction.

      · "S_1Q_3" - wide S in I , large Q in III .

      · Inverted T wave $V_1 \rightarrow V_4$.

      · ST depressed in II .

      · Often transient Right B.B.B.

2. Electrolytes

    A. Increased K^+

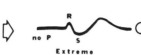

wide, flat P   wide QRS   peaked T   no P   R   S   Extreme

    B. Decreased K^+

flat T   U wave   U   Extreme

    C. Increased Ca^{++}

      short Q-T

    D. Decreased Ca^{++}

      long QT

3. Patterns

    A. Strain

      Left Ventricular: Right Ventricular:

      Lead V_5 Lead V_2

    B. Artificial Pacemaker

    pacemaker spike

miscellaneous Continued

Pericarditis

flat or concave

elevated

Subendocardial Injury

depressed
S T

4. Drug Effects

A. Digitalis (may cause ST depression)

sloping ST

diphasic T

—or—

inverted T

short QT

short QT

Digitalis Excess:

P.A.T. with block, SA block, AV block,

Nodal Tachycardia with A-V dissociation.

Digitalis Toxicity:

P.V.C.'s, Bigeminy,

Ventricular Tachycardia,

Atrial or Ventricular Fibrillation.

B. Quinidine

wide, notched P

wide QT

U wave

wide QRS

ST depression

Roller Coaster pattern of

Quinidine toxicity.

From:

Rapid Interpretation of EKG's

by

Dale Dubin, M.D.

Published by:
COVER Publishing Company*
P. O. Box 1092
Tampa, Florida
* a division of C.O.V.E.R. Inc.

This section contains EKG tracings from various patients (and their interpretation). The tracings and interpretations are provided so that you can see how this method of reading EKG's actually works. Try these few examples so that you will be accustomed to this systematic approach. Once you learn how to systematically read an EKG you will soon become very skilled at routine EKG interpretations.

Patient D.D. is a 29 year old white male known to be a hypochondriac with numerous complaints.

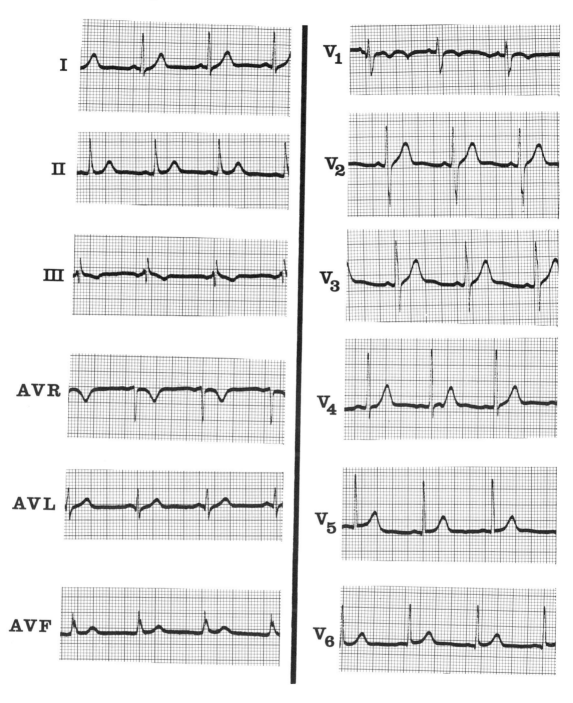

Patient: D.D.

Rate: about 70 per minute

Rhythm: Regular Sinus Rhythm
P-R less than .2 sec. (No A V Block)
QRS less than .12 sec. (No B.B.B.)
... but note the R-R′ in III suggesting incomplete Bundle Branch
Block.

Axis: Normal Range (but slight counter-clockwise rotation in the horizontal
plane).

Hypertrophy: No atrial hypertrophy
No ventricular hypertrophy

Infarction: No significant Q waves
(coronary   ST segments — not elevated, except for V₆ where ST is elevated
vascular   ½ mm.
status)   T waves — generally upright

Comment: This is an essentially normal tracing. This is the author's own
EKG.

Patient R.C. is a 45 year old white male with a history of coronary vascular disease. Blood pressure was 210/100 on admission.

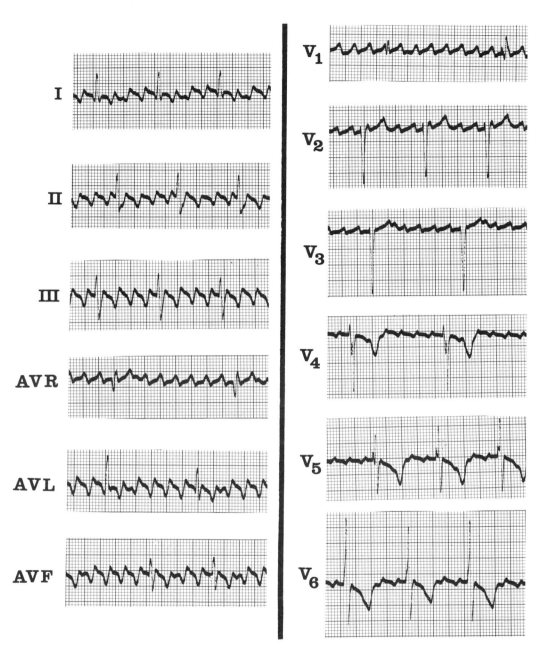

EKG Interpretation

Patient: R.C.

Rate: Atrial rate of 300/minute
      Ventricular rate generally 75/min. but occasionally slower.

Rhythm: Atrial Flutter (with inconsistent ventricular response, i.e. no fixed
              ratio).
      P-R is variable
      QRS is less than .12 sec. (No B.B.B.)

Axis: Vector points directly to patient's left or 0°. Clockwise rotation in the
      horizontal plane.

Hypertrophy: Atrial hypertrophy difficult to determine.
           No ventricular hypertrophy.

Infarction: *Q waves* — significant *Q waves* in I and AVL.
(coronary   *ST segments* are generally isoelectric.
vascular   *T waves* are inverted in V_4, V_5, and V_6.
status)

Comment: This patient has Atrial Flutter. There is evidence of an old lateral
      infarction probably due to a previous occlusion of the Left Cir-
      cumflex Coronary Artery. The inverted T waves probably indicate
      that the coronary arteries are somewhat narrowed.

Patient K.T. is a 61 year old obese male who was brought into the emergency room by his family. This patient had a sudden episode of severe left chest pain. Blood pressure was 100/60.

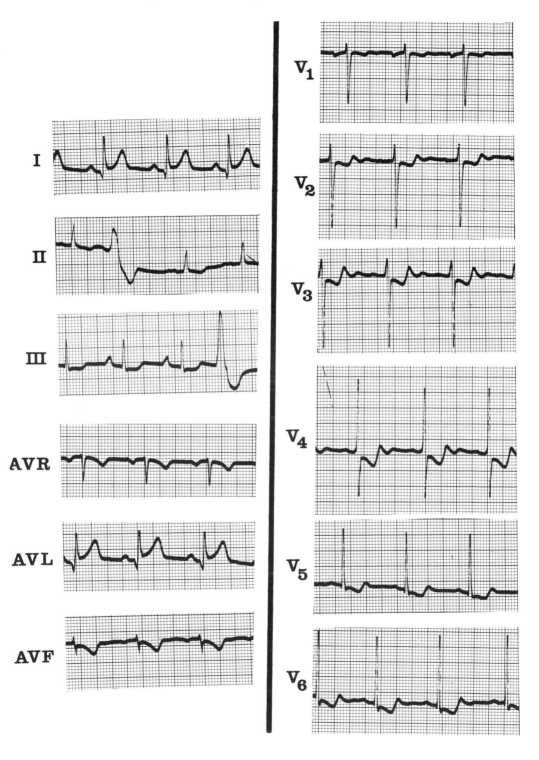

EKG Interpretation

Patient: K.T.

Rate: about 75/minute

Rhythm: Generally Regular Sinus Rhythm with occasional P.V.C.'s.
P-R is exactly .2 sec. so we will have to say there is a borderline first degree A V Block.
QRS — less than .12 second.

Axis: Left Axis Deviation

Hypertrophy: Probable left atrial hypertrophy.
Left ventricular hypertrophy.

Infarction: Significant Q waves in I and AVL.
(coronary ST segments are elevated in I and AVL. ST segments are de-
vascular   pressed in V_1, V_2, V_3, and V_4.
status) T waves are flat or inverted in V_1 through V_6.

Comment: This patient has an acute lateral infarction suggesting occlusion of the Left Circumflex Coronary Artery. Note the prominent R wave and ST depression in the right chest leads (try the mirror test). This suggests an acute posterior infarction as well, so a branch of the Right Coronary Artery may also be involved. This patient has severe ischemic coronary disease as evidenced by the T waves. The Left Axis Deviation may be due to left ventricular hypertrophy.

Patient G.G. is a 45 year old Negro male who was doing heavy work when he was overcome by severe, crushing anterior chest pain. Blood pressure was 110/40 on admission to the hospital.

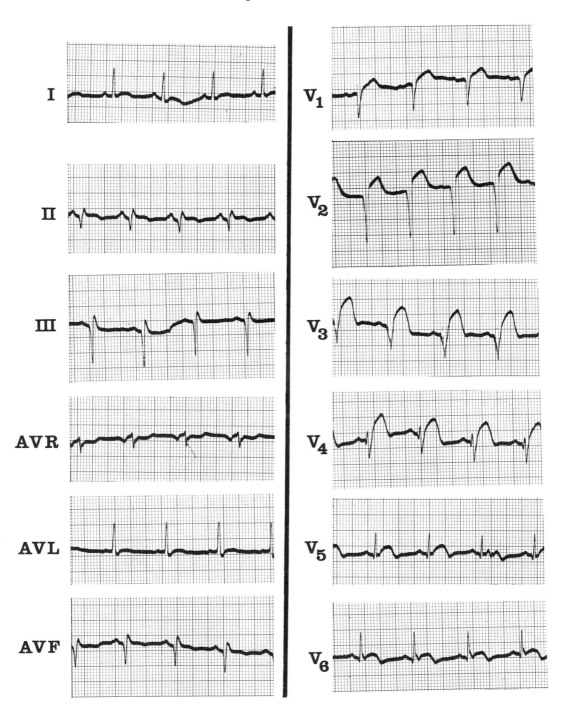

EKG Interpretation

Patient: G.G.

Rate: about 100/min. but variable.

Rhythm: Regular Sinus Rhythm
P-R less than .2 sec. (No A V Block)
QRS less than .12 sec. (No B.B.B.)

Axis: Left Axis Deviation

Hypertrophy: No atrial hypertrophy.
No ventricular hypertrophy.

Infarction: Significant Q *waves* in II, III, and AVF.
(coronary   There are also very large Q waves in V_1, V_2, V_3, and V_4.
vascular   *ST segments* are elevated in V_1, V_2, V_3, and V_4.
status) T *waves* are difficult to distinguish but inverted T waves are noted in V_4, V_5, and V_6.

Comment: This patient has an acute anterior infarction probably representing an occlusion of the Anterior Descending branch of the Left Coronary. The old inferior infarction demonstrated on this EKG was noted on the patient's previous hospital record. Previous EKG's showed no anterior involvement on his last admission.

Patient E.M. is a 65 year old white female. She was admitted to the hospital because of constant left chest pain for twelve hours. Blood pressure on admission was 110/75.

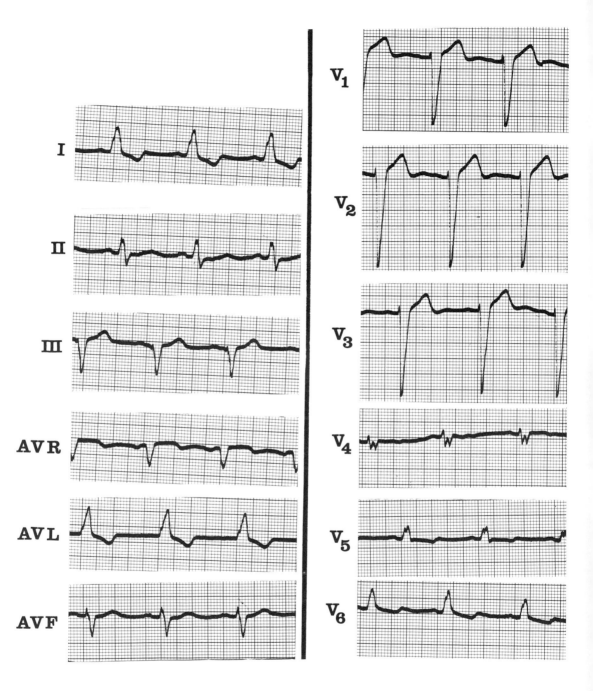

EKG Interpretation

Patient: E.M.

Rate: 60 (Sinus Bradycardia)

Rhythm: Regular Sinus Rhythm
    P-R is about .2 sec. and therefore there is probably a first degree
    A V Block.
    QRS is more than .12 sec. (it is .16 sec. wide).
    R-R′ is present in V_5 and V_6 so there is a Left Bundle Branch
    Block.

Axis: Suggestive of Left Axis Deviation, but not reliable because of the
    presence of Bundle Branch Block.

Hypertrophy: No atrial hypertrophy
    Ventricular hypertrophy is difficult to determine because of
    Bundle Branch Block.

Infarction: *Q Waves* — not a reliable criterion of infarction in the presence
(coronary   of Left Bundle Branch Block.
vascular   *ST segments* not reliable in the presence of Left Bundle
status)   Branch Block.
    T Waves are flat in V_4, V_5, and V_6.

Comment: Vectorcardiogram and enzyme studies confirmed a suspected
    diagnosis of myocardial infarction. A careful study of the pa-
    tient's chest pains made us suspicious.

Patient M.A. is a 75 year old white female with a long history of marked hypertension. This patient was involved in an automobile accident and suffered a comminuted fracture of her left femur. Blood pressure on admission 90/50.

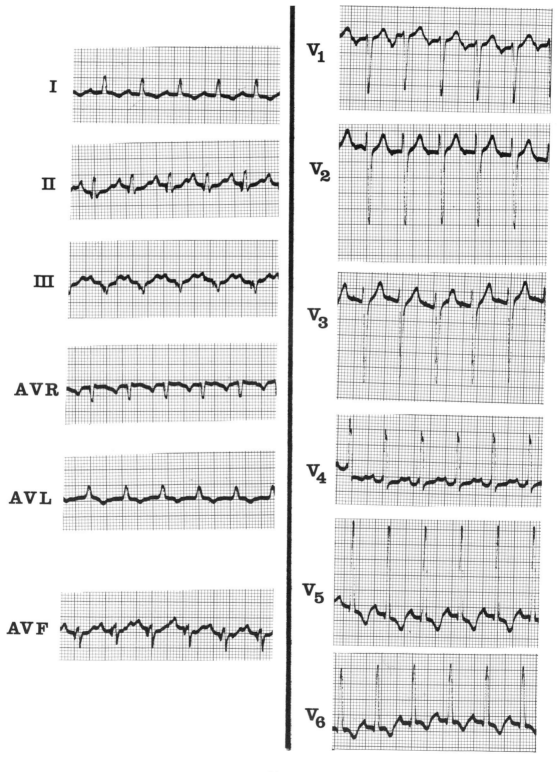

Patient: M.A.

Rate: about 125/minute

Rhythm: Regular Sinus Rhythm
        P-R is less than .2 seconds
        QRS is less than .12 seconds

Axis: Left Axis Deviation

Hypertrophy: Left atrial hypertrophy
             Left ventricular hypertrophy

Infarction: *Q waves* are present in II, III, and AVF.
(coronary   *ST segments* — generally isoelectric (on baseline), but V_5 and
vascular V_6 show "strain" pattern.
status)   *T waves* are inverted in V_5 and V_6.

Comment: This patient was in (hypovolemic) shock as evidenced by heart
rate and blood pressure. This patient has hypertrophy of both
the left atrium and left ventricle with a left ventricular strain
pattern. The patient also had an old inferior infarction.

INDEX